$2.6

THE SECULAR SEARCH FOR A NEW CHRIST

"There are many sincere and enlightened people today for whom Jesus is not a christ.... There are other contemporary christs who have their followers but who are not so formalized in temple and scripture...Mahatma Gandhi, Albert Schweitzer, John F. Kennedy, Martin Luther King, Mao Tse-tung."

GUSTAVE H. TODRANK

The Secular Search for a New Christ

The Secular Search
for a New Christ

by
Gustave H. Todrank

THE WESTMINSTER PRESS
Philadelphia

STANDARD BOOK NO. 664–24858–6
LIBRARY OF CONGRESS CATALOG CARD NO. 73–76992

PUBLISHED BY THE WESTMINSTER PRESS®
PHILADELPHIA, PENNSYLVANIA

PRINTED IN THE UNITED STATES OF AMERICA

TO

Elizabeth
    Stephen and
        Josephine

Preface

TRADITIONAL Christianity is largely irrelevant to the current world situation. For any religion to become and remain a vital force in the lives of a new generation it must be remodeled from time to time. This is especially important in times of rapid and basic social change. Ours are such times, and Christianity has not kept pace.

The purpose of this book is to attempt to reinterpret some of the fundamentals of the Christian tradition. Although the terminology occasionally appears typically Christian, it should be pointed out that the old words are used in new ways which, hopefully, escape the tired provincialism of the past. Since this study was conceived and developed in college classes enrolling Muslim, Jew, Buddhist, and Hindu, it strives to contribute to a dialogue that goes beyond the usual denominational limits. Hence, the natural result is that the more ancient and parochial interpretations of traditional Christianity have given way to a more contemporary and cosmopolitan orientation, a Christianity that is genuinely secular and ecumenical.

The purpose of the book should choose its reading public. It is not designed to disturb those who are satisfied and happy with orthodox convictions. Rather, it is directed to those who are searching for some alternative interpretations that are more directly applicable to the present situation. It does not claim to have *all* the answers for *anyone*, or even *any* answers for *everyone*, but it hopes to offer something of enduring value to those who pursue its course.

The nature of the study is such that it needs to be read in the order in which it is presented. The clarity of each chapter depends upon the contents of the previous ones. For this reason, a detailed Contents is included rather than an index. From it the browser with only casual interest can quickly and reliably discern both the thesis and the structure of the study as a whole. To facilitate transition and discussion the same detailed outline is identified throughout the text.

Acknowledgments are necessarily and admittedly incomplete, but special appreciation is directed to the many students who have been "a refining fire," to Colby College for Sabbatical generosities and other assistance, to the Danforth Foundation for the opportunity to discuss some of these ideas in a seminar at Camp Miniwanca, and to my family for encouragement and patience beyond measure. It goes without saying that none of these benefactors is to be held accountable for what is said here; with each there is spirited disagreement on some of the ideas in some of the chapters. This only invites the author to emphasize all the more that his indebtedness goes far beyond the footnotes and his gratitude far beyond this preface and the text.

G.H.T.

Colby College
Waterville, Maine

Contents

CHAPTER I

The Current Revolution
in Christianity

THE study of history shows that every civilization has times of stability and order on the one hand and times of violence and rapid social change on the other. Each of these extremes can be characterized and dated by the historian. Each is illustrated repeatedly in the development of Biblical literature as the centers of cultural influence pass from one location to another: from Egypt to Assyria, then to Babylonia, then to Persia, then to Greece, and finally to Rome. Our temporal distance from these historic transitions helps us to distinguish the decades of peace and security from the decades of upheaval and revolution.

But even without the benefit of temporal distance from our own times, we recognize the middle of the twentieth century as basically revolutionary. Every area of our common life is being challenged by new and momentous discoveries. The exploitation of atomic and nuclear energy for military purposes has forced upon us a new era in international negotiation. The launching of manned satellites has catapulted us into a new space age. Vast areas of the world seem to be awakening to the opportunity, if not yet the responsibility, of basic civil rights. Spectacular advances in transportation and communication have forced more and more governments to defend their domestic and foreign policies in a court of world opinion. Moreover, in taking advantage of the new developments in communication and transportation many students throughout the world have come to recognize the attitudes of their parents

tion of Christianity, a rebirth of the Christian Word in a new and final form."[1] In *The Secular City*, Harvey Cox indicates that the collapse of traditional religion is one of the two hallmarks of our era and goes on to argue, rightly or wrongly, that we need a "theology of revolution."[2] Bishop John A. T. Robinson begins *Honest to God* with a chapter entitled "Reluctant Revolution" and *The New Reformation?* with a chapter entitled "Troubling of the Waters," in which he indicates clearly that more than a reformation is involved: "It means the dissolution of one world and the birth-pangs of another."[3] These references are typical of a great number of books and articles by scholars of different faiths who agree that the change is revolutionary.

For further support of this thesis one need only observe the extensive and radical change in ethics, liturgy, and social action as well as in theology. If the scope and speed of change in these areas continues at the present pace, the old forms will no longer be evident in the new. Since the odds are in favor of accelerated change, it is more accurate to speak of revolution than reformation.

The Meaning of "Current." To speak of the "current" revolution in Christianity is to imply that this one is not the first. Evidence for earlier revolutions can be found in the arguments suggesting that the religion *of* Jesus becomes a religion *about* Jesus in the writings of Paul, or that the creedal or dogmatic Christian Church embraced doctrines and practices that were totally foreign to Jesus, the Twelve, or Paul. Whether or not the activities of the Anabaptists and the Socinians in the sixteenth century were reformation or revolution must be left to the church historians, but certainly the current revolution is not the first. Indeed, it seems that our present times are several revolutions removed from Biblical times and that it is therefore a very dubious practice to find easy "Biblical sources" in explaining contemporary change. The terminology used here intends to emphasize the *distance from* rather than the similarities with Biblical times. In other words, it is to use the terms "current" and "revolution" as Webster suggests.

Christianity and the Larger Revolution. It goes without saying that the current general revolution involves more than any one religion or any one country, say, Christianity in America. Reports from abroad indicate clearly that other countries and other religions are engaged in similar contest and change. Every aspect of life in every modern country is feeling the effects of the current revolution. In such a situation meaningful discussion requires a focal point.

The word "Christianity" indicates the general locus of concern. It points out the general area under discussion and sets it apart from other general areas such as government or economics or naval warfare. Since the entire study will be given to a new definition of Christianity, no more needs to be said about the term for the moment than that it identifies the focus of interest within a larger revolutionary setting.

2. The Dimensions of the Revolution

Every aspect of Christian thought and action is under attack. The breadth and depth of the assault can be illustrated through a brief discussion of such key symbolic phrases as "theology without God," "christology without Jesus," "Bible without authority," "church without clergy," "salvation without immortality," and "morality without immorality."

Theology Without God. Theology can be interpreted in either a limited etymological sense or in a more broad and general way. In the narrower usage it refers to the study of the nature and existence of deity. The more general usage includes a wider variety of themes having to do with the relationships between God and man.[4] In the latter sense, for example, it would include such topics as creation, revelation, sin and salvation, scripture, religious organization, and so forth. It is sufficient for present purposes to say that theology is the study of the fundamentals of some religious faith, whether it be one world religion or another. Christian theology is concerned with the basic aspects of the Christian faith and tradition.

There have always been those who have questioned the prevailing notions about deity. Some have gone no farther than to insist that the evidence is inconclusive and hence have withheld personal commitment—the agnostics. Others have gone so far as to argue that the evidence is conclusive against the existence of God as traditionally conceived—the atheists. In varying degrees each of these basic points of view has had such notable representatives as Xenophanes, Socrates, Democritus, Nietzsche, and Huxley, to mention only a few.

In our own times there is a new brand of professed atheism. Whereas the atheists of old would generally agree that denying the existence of God refers to the past as well as to the present, the current "death of God" theologian makes a clear distinction between past and present. While God was once present and active in our tradition, now God has died and disappeared. "A theological statement that proclaims the death of God must mean that God is not present in the Word of faith. Insofar as the theologian speaks of the death of God—and actually means what he speaks—he is speaking of the death of God himself."[5] William Hamilton phrases it forcefully: "God is dead. We are not talking about the absence of the experience of God, but about the experience of the absence of God."[6]

Contrary to the earlier atheists who would have thought that the theologian should seek other employment, the radical theologian insists not only that he is a theologian but that he is engaged in pastoral work. Altizer and Hamilton suggest this in the preface to their *Radical Theology and the Death of God.*

> The aim of the new theology is not simply to seek relevance or contemporaneity for its own sake but to strive for a whole new way of theological understanding. Thus it is a theological venture in the strict sense, but it is no less a pastoral response hoping to give support to those who have chosen to live as Christian atheists.[7]

The current popularity of this so-called radical theology suggests that it is making a contribution to our times and hence will continue as a factor in the revolution in Christianity. Thus it is legitimate to use the phrase, silly as it may appear at first, "theology without God."

Strangely enough, as God passes from the central role for

the "death of God" theologian, Jesus appears in a new and ever more important incarnation. But for another group of theologians the centrality of Jesus is very dubious, and this leads to another phase of the current revolution.

Christology Without Jesus. For most Christians the notion of a "christology without Jesus" is as ridiculous as a "theology without God." The reason is not hard to find. Just as theology has a narrow and a broad usage, so also has christology. In the narrow or etymological sense it is the study of the nature and purpose of the christ (messiah); in the broader usage it could include the name and person of the one who is believed to be the christ. The Christian tradition adopted the broader usage so exclusively that it neglected the significance of the distinction. The obvious and unfortunate result was the use of "Jesus" and "Christ" as synonyms.

But it can be shown historically that a clear distinction must be made between "Jesus" and "Christ." "Christ" refers to an aspect of Jewish eschatology, the "messiah" of Jewish expectation. "Jesus" refers to a man, not an "office" or "function." Although it is accurate to say that the office often shapes the man and that the man influences the office, the distinction should not be confused. Moreover, when the distinctions are kept in mind one can readily see that one can have a "christology without Jesus."

Two questions pose the problem succinctly: First, was Jesus of Nazareth a historical person? And secondly, if so, was he the messiah (christ) of Jewish expectation? There is fundamental disagreement on both questions. No New Testament scholar has been able to convince all other New Testament scholars that Jesus was an actual historical figure. Further, some of those scholars who accept the historicity of Jesus deny that he was the christ of Jewish expectation. All the scholars should agree that one can have a "christology without Jesus," but they do not; hence, the debate continues with revolutionary implications.

The Bible Without Authority. For much of traditional Christianity the Bible has been the final authority for the faith.

Anyone who is sympathetic to this point of view would recoil with shock, if not with horror, at the notion of "the Bible without authority." But in the current revolution the authority of the Bible is under heavy fire. Present purposes do not require the examination of the more subtle aspects of Biblical interpretation (hermeneutics). Two brief elementary discussions will illustrate the problem of Biblical authority: the first has to do with the contradictions in the Bible and the second with the inevitability of individual interpretation.

Those who currently challenge the authority of the Bible find reason for doing so by reading it. From the beginning, and all the way through, it is fraught with differences that sometimes amount to flat contradictions. These contradictions involve not only specific details such as who inspired David to take the census (God or Satan), the number of generations between Abraham and Jesus, the list of the twelve disciples, etc., but more fundamental attitudes such as those toward the order of creation, the implications of wealth and work, marriage and divorce, the nature of the covenant, the nature and will of God, and many more. The fact is that some parts of the Bible contradict other parts of the Bible.

A second aspect that challenges Biblical authority is the inevitability of individual interpretation. The fact is that the evangelists and the scholars often disagree on what the Bible says and what it means by what it says. With equal sincerity they can invoke the Holy Spirit to attend their study, and still they find themselves in disagreement. Moreover, each can quote the Bible to his own advantage. The fact that many Christians will deny that there are contradictions in the Bible and then attempt to show that they have schemes for overcoming the perils of individual interpretation is the very reason for including within the scope of the revolution the notion of "the Bible without authority."

Church Without Clergy. Until very recently most Christians would have found the idea of a "church without clergy" as inconceivable as a "Bible without authority." Many still do. The reason for this is that traditional Christianity has acknowledged a marked distinction between two contrasting realms: the natural and the supernatural, the secular and the sacred, the church and the world, the clergy and the laity. Each of these functioned in its own way in contrast with its opposite. The religious aspects of each of these contrasts had a basic affinity with each other; they were interrelated, the supernatural with the sacred, the sacred with the church, the church with the clergy, and so on. The sacrament of ordination related the church and the clergy in a special way. To this way of thinking, a "church without clergy" was incomprehensible.

Now there are rumblings of discontent which suggest that this whole pattern of thought is changing. The extent to which these rumblings are representative of the general citizenry remains to be seen, but some revolutionary ideas are appearing and are apparently receiving a wide and enthusiastic hearing. If these ideas are taken seriously, the result may well be a church without clergy, at least as it has been understood in the past. Naturally the focus of the discussion has to do with the respective roles of the clergy and the laity in the church of the future. Bishop John A. T. Robinson is calling for a "genuinely lay theology."[8] Gibson Winter goes much farther and finds the *"emergence of the laity* as the ministering center of Christianity" and in this the birth of "a new image of the Church—the servanthood of the laity."[9] For Winter, the emerging laity becomes the only possible church and in the end the roles of the clergy and the laity as traditionally understood are abolished.[10]

Since these notions differ significantly from traditional doctrines, and since large numbers of both clergy and laity still prefer the more orthodox interpretations, there is spirited debate about a "church without clergy," and thus reason for including it as one of the aspects of the current revolution in Christianity.

Salvation Without Immortality. Like the other four aspects of the current revolution discussed above, the idea of "salvation without immortality" is incomprehensible to the traditional Christian. The reason is obvious. The Christian attitude toward salvation has always been predominantly otherworldly.

The present world with its threescore years and ten is preparatory for the eternity to follow, and no sacrifice, even torture to martyrdom, is too great a price to pay if it will reap benefits in the life to come. Salvation is the primary concern of Christianity and it is inseparable from the notion of immortality. Hence, the notion of salvation without immortality seems almost a contradiction of terms.

One aspect of the current revolution in Christianity is an obvious transition from the otherworldly to the this-worldly. Widespread doubt of any life after death is clearly a part of this current trend. The old notion of "heaven up there" or "pie in the sky when you die" is associated with the medieval world in the minds of many people today. To question either the reality or the value of a future life is to increase the importance of the present life. Since there is no conclusive evidence either for or against life after death, this study will work itself out independently of any point of view on immortality. But the transition from an otherworldly to a this-worldly orientation has revolutionary consequences, one of which is the notion of salvation without immortality.

Morality Without Immorality. The influence of theology on morality has a long history in the Judeo-Christian tradition. It goes back at least to the time of the transition from the henotheism of Moses to the ethical monotheism of the great Hebrew prophets. Ethical monotheism, as the prophets conceived it, included several significant developments: first, there is only one God; secondly, this one God is ethical in nature; and thirdly, this ethical God expects the moral behavior of man to reflect the ethical nature of God. Moreover, these prophets claimed to be the spokesmen for God, to know not only his nature but also his will. They thought of God as universally just and loving; therefore, man should practice universal justice and love. The resulting morality is well known to both Christian and Jew. Given a God who is omnipotent, omniscient, and omnipresent, who has a plan of salvation for his children individually and collectively, and given a spokesman who can make known to the people the will of the Omni-God, the result is a morality based on eternal principles and universal absolutes, forever relevant in every place and for any occasion. (This is the old morality.)

With such a close relationship between theology and morality, a revolution in one is certain to produce corresponding change in the other. Without an attempt to suggest which of these is more influential than the other, it can be acknowledged without hesitation that a new morality is challenging the old at the very cornerstone of Sinai and the Covenant. It does not accept the prophetic "Thus saith Yahweh" approach because it does not accept either Yahweh or his prophet. Nor does it accept the necessity of eternal principles or universal absolutes. Like the old, it is concerned with the details of Christian behavior and often agrees on what Christians ought to do, but the difference appears when one attempts to justify one's actions. Whereas the old morality appeals to the will of God, the Bible, or some other form of absolute, the new morality appeals to the opportunities and demands of love in the "situation." The new morality insists on being free to examine the relevant aspects of the current situation and to make decisions accordingly. Since the situations of life vary from time to time and place to place, creative ethics must be "situation ethics" rather than ethics based on presumed eternal absolutes.[11]

Naturally, there is spirited difference of opinion about "old" and "new." Some are quick to question whether the new morality is either "new" or "morality." Others could point out that the new morality is getting rid of immorality in the transition from "sin" to "sickness" to "situation." The changes in attitudes toward homosexuality probably best illustrate the transition. In the Old Testament, homosexuality is clearly regarded as sinful and punishable by death. More recent psychologists have diagnosed homosexuality as sickness. Now ethicists and jurists can condone private homosexual relations between consenting adults if the situation justifies them. If one ponders the implications of the transition from "sin" to "sickness" to "situation," does this not mean that one can have "morality without immorality"? The debate continues with revolutionary consequences.

Conclusion: No Area Will Escape. A preliminary two-part conclusion can be drawn. First, no area of Christian thought or life can long escape the most careful and penetrating scrutiny. There is no part of life that is not touched by either theology or morality. But what is new and significant here is not the fact of challenge and change but rather the scope and speed of challenge and change. Hence, one must conclude, secondly, that we are truly in the midst of a revolution the consequences of which largely elude us. There is no question about this conclusion in the mind of Bishop Robinson when he writes in *The New Reformation?*

> I would say that the very fact that the basic truth of Christianity is itself at issue, that even God is at hazard, and that nothing is being left unquestioned, is surely a sign that a new thing is upon us. This is not just a continuation of planned reform.[12]

If we truly are in the midst of such a far-reaching revolution, there must be some basic discontent that is giving rise to it. The next section will attempt to identify some of the causes of the current revolution.

3. THE CAUSES OF THE REVOLUTION

Like every revolution in history, the current one in Christianity is rooted in some fundamental dissatisfaction. For the most part, the revolutionaries have come from within the ranks where the expectations have been highest and the disenchantment deepest. Both clergy and laity are involved. Hence, the complaints should not be dismissed lightly as if originating from those whose wisdom and motivation are in question. The more formidable objections to traditional Christianity include an obsolete theology, a questionable ethics, an antiquated liturgy, and dubious institutional practices. Each of these merits brief comment.

An Obsolete Theology. In traditional Christianity, God has been thought of as a kind and loving Heavenly Father, an *omni* and an *only* God. As *omni*potent, God could do anything and everything, even feats that escaped our comprehension, such as parting a sea or turning sticks into snakes or restoring a corpse to life. As *omni*scient, God knew everything, even my most secret thoughts and the results of events that had not yet happened. As *omni*present, God was everywhere, even nearer to me than parts of my body. His presence and power were manifested from time to time through miraculous interventions on behalf of the faithful. Prayer to this God could heal the sick and move mountains. As an *only* God he had no legitimate competition. All other gods of all other religions were phony idols.

This conception of God simply does not square with human experience. Too frequently the prayers of the faithful go unnoticed; sickness and mountains remain. Too frequently the wicked prosper while the righteous perish. For a long time the orthodox faithful gave this God the benefit of the doubt on the assumption that they probably were too stupid and sinful to understand his marvelous ways. That day is now largely past, and that notion of God is disappearing. Clearly it must be replaced with a conception that is more viable to the current scene.

Similarly, the traditional interpretation of Jesus is in need of revision. The Christian Church has transformed a *man* from Nazareth into the second person of the Trinity, a *deity* who is both fully man and fully God. The fact is that Jesus was a man, a man of his own times. As a man of his times he believed with others that David wrote all the psalms, that demon possession was the cause of illness, that the end of the age was at hand, and so on. From the Dead Sea Scrolls it is evident that he was influenced by the teachings of the Essenes, a contemporary sect that predated Jesus by at least two centuries. Although these beliefs may have been helpful to people then, we know now that they are not only obsolete, they are false. The honest contemporary Christian must be willing to face the possibility that the teachings of Jesus about God, prayer, sin, and salvation may be as unreliable as his beliefs about the cause of illness or the end of the age. Before the contemporary Christian can preach Jesus to his fellowmen he must find something in the

and grandparents as provincial and obsolete. Widespread willingness, even eagerness, to experiment with both new machines and new patterns of behavior reveals that ours are times of turmoil and transition. No area of our common life will long escape.

The concern of this introductory chapter is restricted to a specific part of this much larger revolution, that is, to the current revolution in Christianity. In the interests of clarity the chapter is divided into sections which introduce the theme and define the key terms, identify the dimensions and causes of the revolution, and finally preview an attempt at a creative response.

1. INTRODUCING THE THEME

It is appropriate in this introduction to the theme of the chapter to explain the usage of the key words in the title, namely, why the term "revolution" is being used, what is meant by "current," and the restrictive usage of the term "Christianity."

Revolution or Reformation? Each of these terms signifies change. In a religious context reformation usually refers to change that eliminates faults by either returning to a preferable previous condition or by developing a new principle or practice. In a reformation the older forms are still detectable in the new. Revolution refers to change that is so drastic in scope and speed that the older forms are deliberately destroyed lest they delay the adoption of the new. The distinction being made here between revolution and reformation has to do primarily with the scope and the speed of the change. No one can deny that there is rapid basic change in Christianity. The question is, Is it reformation or revolution?

The evidence seems to favor revolution. One could point first to some of the more vocal and articulate young theologians who claim to be involved in a revolution. Thomas J. J. Altizer suggests in *The Gospel of Christian Atheism* that "the radical Christian is a revolutionary, he is given to a total transforma-

precept or example of Jesus that is both unique to Jesus and relevant to the current situation. Tragic as it may at first appear to the traditional Christian, the relevant aspects of the teachings of Jesus are not unique to him, and the unique aspects are now largely irrelevant, if not inaccurate. In evangelism, enthusiasm is not an adequate substitute for homework, and Christian evangelism needs to take another look at the records.

Another theological aspect in the causes of the current revolution is the inadequacy of the Bible. Any objections to the Bible must be made in terms of its own intent. If it made no claims to relevance to the lives of people today, one could accept it for what it is, a body of literature depicting a long evolutionary development of a religious tradition. But the fact is that it claims both authority and finality over every time and place, each of these being rooted in the more basic claim of being the words and the Word of God. These claims are both general and specific. (Ex. 19:9; Isa. 59:21; Ezek. 43:7 f.; Matt. 5:18–19; John 14:6; I Cor. 3:11; Heb. 13:8; and Rev. 22:18–19.)

Current scholarship will not sustain either of the claims. The claim to authority is compromised by both the internal contradictions and the inevitability of individual interpretations. Indeed, the internal contradictions are themselves evidence of the role of individual interpretation of time and place in the development of this literature. Nor will current scholarship support the claim of finality. Just as those who wrote it reflect their time and place, so also we who read it do the same. The very fact that there never has been a consensus of interpretation suggests transitoriness rather than finality. Moreover, the various Biblical conceptions of man and his relations to God and nature are foreign to the more relevant and reliable notions today. Hence, the contents of the Bible are no more relevant or reliable than the interpretive abilities of the reader.

The Christian Church has made identical claims, and for identical reasons its claims must be rejected and denounced. Any honest reading of the records will show a variety of interpretations as the centuries come and go, and the abuses of authority in the exercising of its assumed power are evident in tortured mind and martyred flesh. Reading the history of the Christian Church requires a steady nerve and a strong stomach. The roles of both the altar and the pulpit need careful reconsideration.

But the point at which the obsolescence of traditional Christian theology is most evident is in its scheme of salvation. The Christian myth of salvation takes place in a three-story world with heaven above, earth beneath, and hell under the earth. It begins with a rebellion in heaven, the beginning of a continuing contest between Satan and God, during which some angels fall. To restore the depleted heavenly ranks, God creates Adam and Eve in the Garden of Eden, innocent and righteous. But, tempted by Satan through a serpent, Adam and Eve disobey a command of God and are driven from the garden by an angel, losing their innocent state. Thereafter they will know trial and pain, and their descendants will be born in sin and deserving of damnation. His purpose thus thwarted, in time God comes to earth in the form of his Son, born as the baby Jesus to the Virgin Mary. Jesus grows to manhood with unusual wisdom and miraculous powers. He gathers to himself twelve disciples and they go about the countryside doing marvelous deeds and preaching God's will. The political and religious authorities take offense, and Jesus is tried and crucified. Through it all, Jesus remains sinless and hence his death is the perfect sacrifice appeasing God's wrath and restoring his honor, gaining for man potential redemption. On the third day Jesus is miraculously raised from the dead. After a divine commission to his disciples he ascends into heaven, from which he will soon return. In the meantime the disciples establish the church as the divine institution for showing men how to win actual redemption when the Son returns to earth again for the final day of judgment. In the judgment, the righteous will be rewarded with eternal bliss with God in heaven while the evil ones will be damned to an eternal suffering with Satan in a hell of fire, concluding God's glorious plan of salvation.[13]

In detail this myth of salvation may be unique, but in its fundamentals it is very similar to the salvation myths of other world religions and of the mystery religions. In these other myths we find references, for example, to a divine descent, incarnation, virgin birth, heralding angels and attending shepherds, choosing of disciples, sharing a last fellowship supper, violent death, resurrection from the dead, ascension into heaven, and so forth. Like the others, the Christian myth is the result of a number of influences that were felt in the culture of the times.

And like the others, the Christian myth of salvation is obsolete for the twentieth century. Its notions of God, man, and salvation are totally foreign to the current way of thinking. To utilize them, man is required to divide himself into duo-membership in the apparently conflicting worlds of the secular and the sacred, of science and religion. Since the myth of salvation is obsolete, and since it involves every aspect of theology, it is probable that the whole of Christian theology needs careful revision.

If this is true of Christian theology, one cannot help wondering whether it is true of other aspects of the Christian life as well.

A Questionable Ethics. Ethics is usually understood as the study of standards of conduct and moral judgment. Christian ethics is the study of Christian standards of behavior. Christian ethics is questionable in two different ways. First, what is meant by "Christian" when one speaks of Christian ethics? A specific and peculiar meaning may be found in one of several ways. First, it may refer specifically to the precept and example of Jesus of Nazareth in that he is called the "Christ." In this case his life and teachings serve as the permanent standard by which a follower would guide his thought and deed. Secondly, it may refer to ethics based on the New Testament as a whole in that it is the canon of "Christian" literature and hence contains the standards of conduct. Thirdly, "Christian" may take its meaning from the teachings of the traditional Christian Church in that it claims Jesus, the New Testament, and the continuing revelation as its basic authority. But each of these choices involves serious difficulties. Not only are the scholars unable to agree on a reliable text in each case; they find in each case that there are conflicting prescriptions for ideal behavior. Hence, the puzzlement.

Secondly, Christian ethics is questionable in the area of relevance. Even if the scholars were able to agree on the text of a Jesus or New Testament ethics, what are the chances that it would be relevant to our times? Both Jesus and the early church believed in an imminent end of the age when everything would change. Hence, any ethics that applied to the interim period would be an interim ethics at best. Further, there is no question but that our age is removed from the interim period by several revolutions. Thus it seems safe to conclude that any ethics that is unique and relevant to those times is not likely to be relevant to our own, and that we had better stop speaking of *Christian* ethics until we can find some specific meaning and application of the term to the twentieth century.

An Antiquated Liturgy. Liturgy here refers to the orderly sequence of worship activities when one finds himself in the midst of the Divine. In the Judeo-Christian tradition man's behavior is supposed to reflect his deepect convictions about God and the good. His behavior in his temple is presumed to be the most revealing. The liturgy of the temple is designed to encourage man's encounter with and facilitate his expressions of the profoundest experiences of life. But in most places of worship today the liturgy is regimented around a theology and morality that is obviously identified with a long-gone yesterday. The readings, prayers, litanies, collects, and too often the sermons are geared to an age that is past. The tragic result is that the keen anticipations of divine encounter all too often yield no more than crucifying disappointment. The fact that so little of profound meaning happens in the sanctuaries today is no small part of the current revolution. The new generation is finding its temples and establishing its worship elsewhere.

Dubious Institutional Practices. Early in its historical development Christianity became institutionalized through an organized church. Even before the end of New Testament times the church believed that it was divinely established and commissioned to serve as God's agency of salvation on earth. In its efforts to achieve its goals it has resorted to some very dubious practices, some of the more obvious of which include a private school system that constantly tries to utilize the public tax treasury; "Christian" businesses which make wine or bread or chocolates, or bind books—to mention only a few—for profit in a competitive market but operate with the distinct advantages of having many captive customers and of paying less taxes or no taxes at all; religious organizations that purchase large lovely estates which then become tax exempt and thereby increase the tax burdens of the neighbors; church-sponsored lobby groups, and so on. These are some of the obvious deliberate abuses.

Then, there are the more unconscious practices with consequences even more subtle and tragic. Serious scholars point out that traditional Christianity can be shown to be "life denying" as well as life affirming, that it involves a "cult of suffering" which seems to thrive both on persecuting and on being persecuted, that it has exploited man's susceptibility to feelings of guilt and has been more concerned with the intensity of beliefs than with their truth.[14]

Conclusion: A Crisis for Christianity. If the discussion of the dimensions of the revolution is accurate, and if this brief survey of some of the causes of the revolution is relevant, then clearly, Christianity is facing a real crisis. With increasing frequency one hears sincere and competent Christian theologians referring to "the world come of age" and "the post-Christian era." There is no doubt that the second half of the twentieth century is a time of revolutionary transition. The language here has been cautious to avoid alienating the traditional Christian. Many students would urge that the charge be stronger: that Christian theology is not merely obsolete, but false; that Christian morality is not merely questionable, but detrimental; that liturgy is is not only antiquated, but stifling; and that the institutional practices mentioned above are not dubious, but rather foul and despicable. Whatever the language, the fact is that more and more people are finding traditional Christianity unsatisfactory for a number of different reasons. The problem is whether or not one can fashion a challenging alternative.

4. ATTEMPTING A CHALLENGING ALTERNATIVE

Attempts to reform are not new to the Judeo-Christian tradition. There were many periods when the attempts were so slow in appearing that hundreds suffered unjust torture and martyrdom, but the fact is that it has been a self-reforming tradition. Several significant illustrations can be found in Biblical literature itself. The second commandment of Moses suggested that God punished the children for the sins of the fathers. Both Jeremiah and Ezekiel specifically denounce the idea. (Jer. 31:29–30; Ezek. 18:1–4.) Jeremiah proposed further that the old covenant of Moses be replaced with a new covenant (Jer., ch. 31) and Jesus suggested that some of the religious patterns established by Ezekiel and Ezra needed to be revised (Matt. 5:21–44). Additional attempts at reform have been made in official church councils and creeds. When Pope John XXIII called the Second Vatican Council "to bring the Church up to date" he was continuing a tradition established long ago. Luther and Calvin were not the first to leave the church in an attempt to reform it, and it may well be that some of the heretics burned at the stake, such as Servetus, may leave to man the nobler legacy. Indeed, is not every thoughtful study of Christianity an attempt to relate the tradition to the times or the times to the tradition? Hence, it is neither new nor arrogant to suggest that the time has come to attempt another basic reform.

Before we attempt a challenging alternative, however, a word needs to be said about the necessity for such an alternative, its criteria for adequacy, and the synopsis of the study as a whole.

The Need for an Alternative. From the sympathetic approach to both the dimensions and the causes of the current revolution, it will not be surprising at this point to find that this study considers the basic orientation of traditional Christianity to be irrelevant to the modern world. The extent of the irrelevance has led to the use of the term "revolution" rather than "reformation." By the same token the language here suggests that something more than reform is required. Modern man needs an *alternative* that is more adequate to his time and place.

The Criteria for Adequacy. It goes without saying that if such an alternative is essential and forthcoming, it will not be traditional, Biblical, doctrinal, nor dogmatic in the usual sense. The assumption here is that it must of necessity go beyond these criteria because they are part of the problem, not criteria for the solution. Hence, criticisms of the study on these bases are irrelevant. This does not mean that this study denies that there is any value in any of these. What it does deny is that any or all of them can be used for measuring the adequacy of a proposed alternative.

On the other hand, the study does aim for clarity, coherence, inclusiveness, relevance, and a degree of novelty. It hopes to be interesting and challenging. In no sense does it claim to be either authoritative or final. It tries to be empirical, though it does not claim to be objective in the sense that it has escaped the influence of the biographical. In the final analysis its adequacy depends upon the extent to which it makes a creative contribution to the life of its reader.

Synopsis of the Study as a Whole. This is a study of secular christian salvation. Each of these terms is used in a specific way, and much of the effort will be given to explain the interpretation. The primary concern and the pivotal notion is salvation, so the next chapter attempts to lay the foundation through a discussion of "the quest for secular salvation." As defined here, salvation often seems to require an agent or christ, so the third chapter defines and analyzes the role of "the secular christ as savior." The fourth chapter attempts to give a soteriological definition of the church and indicates its peculiar function in the continuing experience of salvation. The fifth chapter briefly identifies "the secular community as christian," that is, showing how it should participate in the soteriological scheme. Since no responsible study of christian salvation could omit a discussion of "God and the secular christian life," the sixth chapter undertakes that task. The concluding chapter explores "the secular christian mission in the contemporary world."

CHAPTER II

The Quest for
Secular Salvation

THE preceding chapter attempted to show that a significant revolution is taking place in Christianity, a revolution so extensive that no area of our common life will long escape. The revolution is rooted in some legitimate fundamental objections to Christian theology, ethics, liturgy, and some dubious institutional practices. Although it acknowledged that previous attempts have been made to meet previous objections and that contemporary attempts are being made at the present time, it concluded that the current situation calls for a constructive revolutionary alternative.

This chapter will lay the foundation for one alternative by suggesting that "the quest for secular salvation" is the best place to begin. Since each of the chapters that follow will develop in more detail some of the notions that appear here, it is especially important to be clear at this point. In this effort it is necessary to give a preliminary orientation, to characterize the quest itself, to establish the secular emphasis, and to identify the fundamentals in salvation as here defined.

1. PRELIMINARY ORIENTATION

Following the pattern of the first chapter, the second opens with some preliminary remarks and definitions that should help to clarify the point of departure. These are essential because this study will use some traditional words in nontraditional ways. To achieve the desired orientation at the outset, note the interdependence of the central themes in religion, salvation as the point of departure, the general definition of salvation, and the meaning of "quest."

The Relation of the Central Themes in Religion. To engage in dialogue on any of the central themes in religion—God, Christ, church, sin, salvation, prayer, and so on—is to discover a basic interdependence among them. What one believes about one of these seems to influence what one can believe about the others. For example, one cannot talk about prayer without some explanatory reference to God, because prayer has been understood as conversation directed to God. One cannot talk about redemption without some statement about sin, and by the same token, discussion of sin usually assumes an explanatory reference to God. If one uses these terms in new ways, it is all the more important to make the usage explicit to avoid confusion, but even then the central themes are found to be interdependent. Hence, to establish one idea is to lay the foundation for other ideas that seem to follow from it, and to discredit any hypothesis is to challenge any hypothesis that is based upon it. From this it follows that our reasoning is clearly circular. The problem is achieving a diameter and circumference that is adequate to the need at hand.

The next problem is where to begin. Having acknowledged the interdependence of the central themes and having admitted that attitudes toward any one clearly influence attitudes toward all the others within the circle, where does one enter the circle? One aims at simplicity, consistency, and completeness; one hopes for a world view. But where does one begin to focus his attention?

Salvation as the Point of Departure. At the outset, the point of departure seems arbitrary, either in philosophy or in religion. Stephen Pepper has shown in *World Hypotheses* that there are four or five genuine possibilities in philosophy, any one of which excludes all the others, but no one of which can show conclusively that it is to be preferred over all the others.[15] The point of departure varies with the point of view. The same is true in religion. One may begin with revelation, with God, with man, or as this study does, with the notion of salvation. The extent to which this is either helpful or convincing must be left to the reader to decide at the end of the book. He must wait until the end because the whole study is required to explain the point of departure. This study begins with salvation because it seems to serve as a better guide than any other theme in religion. This chapter and those which follow will show in more detail why this claim is made.

What, then, is meant by salvation?

General Definition of Salvation. The word "salvation" is *not* used here in its traditional sense. To avoid misunderstanding, it should be emphasized that the word needs to be purged of certain parochial connotations. Without intending to offend anyone or to deny anyone the use of the term, "salvation" is *not* used here in the evangelical or Salvation Army sense. Its usage here requires that it be disassociated from any of the so-called salvation cults and understood instead in its earlier and more generic form including "preservation from loss" and "initiation to newness of life," as "profound satisfaction and transforming fulfillment."

"Salvation" refers to a type and quality of experience with two identifiable aspects. First, and more obviously, it refers to those transient experiences of intense meaning, the moments of mystic awareness, the exultation of rapture and ecstasy, the "mountaintop" experiences that daze us momentarily and then create in us a haunting longing to return to the mountain. The place becomes a "holy space" and the hour a "holy time."[16] Like Jacob of old, we, symbolically, build holy altars of sacred stones, *monuments,* to mark the place and recall the time. The notion of a monument suggests another aspect of salvation.

Secondly, not only are we referring to the fleeting moment of "beholding," we are including as well the enduring state of being that follows and abides, the memory of the mountain that lingers and later enlightens the valley of the shadow, affording in the long run an abiding sense of fulfillment or deep satisfaction in everyday living. As we will see, this second aspect will require personal integration and social orientation;

it refers to that specific and general life orientation which gives genuine meaning to each and every phase of our common life, even in the absence of any "beatific vision."

The Meaning of "Quest." One hardly needs to speak of the quest explicitly because its meaning is implicit in the experiences mentioned. How can one, at the mountaintop, sit and *not* sing or stand and *not* dance? The songs and dances are man's natural responses to the beholding of the Beyond in his midst. One never forgets such an encounter. To recall it is to pursue it. Hence the naturalness of the quest.

The quest is itself a vital part of the salvation process. Evolving and dynamic, it thrusts from behind in memory and lures from before in expectation, leaving us, as Augustine found, eternally restless. Thus does the quest itself prepare us, zestful crusaders and chanting pilgrims, for a new glimpse of the Beyond. But the quest, as here defined, should be understood to include the daily routines of our common life as well as the more unusual and romantic beholding of the Divine. Some of the experiences of profoundest fulfillment result from long orientation with the kitchen, or the classroom, or the factory, or the field.

2. The Characteristics of the Quest

Because the quest for salvation is so central in this study and because there are probably many who question its present usage, it is necessary to point explicitly to some of the reasons for making it so pivotal. This can be done by identifying some of the characteristics of the quest.

The Quest as Universal. Every aspect of our deliberate behavior reflects that man is engaged in a quest for salvation in a variety of ways. The language will vary from discipline to discipline but the quest is evident nevertheless. For example, the classic documents that have shaped our political life depict explicitly the hopes and dreams of our founding fathers: the inalienable right to "life, liberty, and the pursuit of happiness." The same vision inspired the eloquent speeches of the late Adlai

E. Stevenson and John F. Kennedy. Moreover, the articulate businessman can demonstrate with passion and persuasion how the aspects of free enterprise in our capitalistic economy are directly related to the same political ideals reflected in the campaigns of statesmen. Men of medicine are motivated by desire for a society without disease, even as are the social scientists. The fine arts usually introduce an idea or feeling that is essential to the aesthetic life. In no area is the quest for salvation more evident than in the literature of the world religions. The fact is that the quest for salvation is universal among men.

The Quest as Eternal. The universality of man's quest for salvation is not new. It is rooted in the records of human history, whether in the areas of government, business, medicine, art, or philosophy and religion. The scriptures of the Judeo-Christian tradition illustrate its historical dimension. Moses was both father and son of a promise, and his followers were pilgrims en route to a land flowing with milk and honey. Amos anticipated the abolition of injustice in "the day of Yahweh" when the Lord would fulfill the dream of his fathers. Isaiah saw destruction coming but believed that a remnant would rise out of the rubble to serve as the creative nucleus for a new Zion. Along with the notion of a remnant was that of a coming messiah. Some eight centuries later the teachings of Jesus were centered in "the kingdom of God" and those of Paul in the parousia. The quest for salvation is central to every era in both the Old and the New Testament.

The quest is eschatological as well as historical, involving the future as well as the past. According to the tradition, God has been active in history, but even more important is the hope and assurance that God will continue to act in order to consummate the historic salvation process in the end of time. Moses did not live to enter the promised land, nor did Amos see "the day of Yahweh." Isaiah did not observe the rising remnant as creative nucleus for the new Zion, nor did Jesus live to see "the kingdom of God." Each of these great prophets died in the hope that the quest would be fulfilled in God's own time. Hence, the quest as eschatological.

To characterize the quest as eternal, identifying its historical and eschatological aspects, is to suggest that it evolves and functions in and through time. It is a process and a pilgrimage that never ends in this life. Along the way there are glimpses that sustain and propel. In those moments when the quest is fulfilled with ineffable satisfaction, there is a dimension of experience which assures one that something sifts from the passing scene everything that is precious and preserves it in its most creative form through all eternity. Perhaps the moments of the quest fulfilled, alone, sustain the universe in its course of eternal creative evolution. Hence, our primary emphasis here is not simply on the quest as fulfilled but more on the notion of continuing growth, the quest as fulfill*ed* when most fulfill*ing*.

The Quest as Clue to Man. If every aspect of deliberate human behavior in every place and time reflects a quest for salvation, perhaps it may serve as a clue to understanding man. As defined earlier, the quest is constitutive of man's being, as both guide and thrust to his life, something that is central in both his memory and his expectation, each of which is prerequisite to the growth of man. Some recent developments in psychotherapy are especially revealing.

Viktor E. Frankl has established a new school of psychotherapy which he calls "logotherapy." The word "logotherapy" comes from the Greek word *logos*, which Frankl translates as "meaning." While Freudian psychoanalysis is centered in a "will to pleasure" and Adlerian psychology in a "will to power," logotherapy emphasizes the *will to meaning*. It "focuses on the meaning of human existence as well as on man's search for such a meaning. According to logotherapy, this striving to find meaning in one's life is the primary motivational force in man."[17] If the will to meaning encounters prolonged "existential frustration," man will develop "noogenic neuroses." "Noogenic neuroses do not emerge from conflicts between drives and instincts but rather from conflicts between various values; in other words, from moral conflicts, or, to speak in a more general way, from spiritual problems."[18] Thus, unless man actually experiences in the living of his daily life the gradual fulfillment of his will to meaning, he will develop neuroses and not function as a wholesome man. Frankl has found ample clinical evidence to support his theory of logotherapy, often discovering that it is effective after other types of psychotherapy have failed.

While Frankl's language is different from that used here, his clinical evidence supports the soteriological thesis of this study. The quest for salvation, or search for meaning, is a clue to understanding man in his individual personal life and in his social relationships. The role of the temporal in logotherapy helps to make transition to the secular emphasis.

3. THE SECULAR EMPHASIS

To speak of the quest for salvation as universal or eternal, or even as the clue to understanding man, is to use an idiom that naturally lends itself to religious language. The terminology is not foreign or unfamiliar and the illustrations seem to follow naturally. But when one moves to a secular orientation he runs the risk of misunderstanding because of the traditional usage of the term "secular." This section will give a preliminary definition of the term, distinguish between the otherworldly and the worldly, attempt a secular mean between the extremes, and conclude with a brief comment relating the quest and personal immortality.

The Meaning of "Secular." Just as the term "salvation" has to be purged from some pejorative connotations, so also must the term "secular." It comes from the Latin *saeculum*, which means "of this time or age" or "related to this world." The history of its usage includes interpretations that were anti-church, antireligious, and antitranscendental. In this study it will be used in its original meaning with no derogatory connotations whatever. It simply means oriented around the present world, having to do with our own life and time. Each of the following topics in this section will help to clarify further how the term is being used.

The Otherworldly and the Worldly. These are familiar terms in religious literature. To speak of a religion as otherworldly suggests that it finds its essential meaning and promise of fulfillment in a world other than the present one. Salvation is reserved for some distant place and some future time, there and then, "there" usually referring to heaven or some ethereal paradise far, far away, and "then" referring to some distant future time after death, or the Judgment Day, or some other cataclasmic event which separates this world from the other. In contrast, a this-worldly orientation emphasizes the importance of the here and now. It tends to minimize the significance of any foreordained mythological cataclasm that is supposed to separate this world and the next, and it denies the validity of the notion that suffering in this life will help to accumulate bliss in the next.

Traditional Christianity has been characteristically otherworldly. The New Testament clearly depicts a world view involving an imminent end of the age. The new aeon, soon to be established through the parousia, would abide for eternity as the kingdom of God, affording eternal bliss in heaven for the righteous and eternal punishment in hell for the damned. Since New Testament times the traditional Christian Church has been largely otherworldly with both a theology and an ethics oriented around the notions of heaven and hell. In these terms the present world of threescore years and ten is little more than a proving ground for the eternity that is to follow.

The Secular Mean Between the Extremes. Both the otherworldly and the this-worldly orientations have inherent dangers. Unless tempered with good judgment the otherworldly approach may lead from wholesome asceticism to actual self-abuse on the assumption that suffering in this life will help to increase the bliss in the next. On the other hand, this-worldly orientations must guard against excessive preoccupation with the here and now to the exclusion of a predictable and beneficial there and then, or to an overemphasis on the importance of man's role and ability. Obviously, some sort of golden secular mean between the extremes must be derived.

The secular christianity of this study attempts a modified this-worldly approach. It is primarily concerned with the here and now, but neither of these is interpreted in some arbitrary fragmentary sense. "Here" refers to where I am, my individual and personal existence. But "here" does not arbitrarily exclude "there." I am not an island in space that is unaffected by the environment around me. So "here" must include my family or tribe, even my society and culture. Indeed, in the final analysis, it must include my universe.

By the same token, "now" means now and not "then," but not in some hard-and-fast momentary sense. Just as we cannot draw distinct lines between the here and there, so also we cannot make inflexible distinctions between the now and then. Salvation involves the intense and mysterious beholding in an overwhelming *now*, which in turn abides to haunt and lure until it seems to become a *then*. Just as we are not islands in space, so also we are not interrupted moments in time. The actual horizons of "now" will depend upon the ability and focus of the individual, but in all cases it clearly involves past, present, and future.

In the quest for secular salvation these three more or less arbitrary temporal divisions of one's awareness are integrally related. If satisfaction or fulfillment is to have any meaning it must have meaning at some point in what is called the present tense. If it forever fails to be *present*, it forever fails. But just as obviously, both the past as remembered and the future as anticipated lay the foundation for the present. Today's deeds are tomorrow's memories of yesterday. Hopes for tomorrow may well be the first step in the fulfillment of today. Salvation in the present tense means, initially, living today in such a way that on the morrow we can remember the past without remorse and anticipate the future without fear. The present should be the crowning glory of the past and the creative potentiality for the future. Even a minimal notion of salvation involves orientation of our lives in space and time. Unless and until satisfaction is gained in this minimal sense of here and now, it is not salvation.

The Secular Quest and Personal Immortality. As indicated earlier, this study neither affirms nor denies immortality. It acknowledges cogent arguments both for and against but insists that the evidence is inconclusive in that no theory or combination of theories is sufficiently persuasive to convince the scholars one way or the other. The point of view assumed here is a pragmatic agnosticism. William James is undoubtedly right when he suggests that in cases where the evidence is inconclusive one may believe in any way that most fulfills his life as long as the belief does not go contrary to established fact. If a person is able to realize greater dimensions of meaning by affirming an acceptable possibility, let it be done. It may be that the attitude assumed will facilitate the gathering of convincing evidence.

But one point is basic to the secular emphasis: the meaning of salvation can be and should be independent of one's notion of life after death. If there is a life after death, the best preparation for it is the best life here and now irrespective of it. The future must function in the abundant living of the present, however each of these is defined. But the interpretation of the future must be limited to the anticipatable or one falls into the trap of otherworldliness. Is not the best preparation for any future, near or far, the quest for secular salvation in the secular here and now?

4. The Fundamentals in Salvation

Now that we have defined and characterized the quest and established the secular emphasis, it is essential to identify some of the fundamentals in salvation. These include the role of the environment, the agent in the salvation process, and the notion of salvation as a gift of Grace. Each of these will feature significantly in the chapters that follow. Hence, the discussion here will be introductory and brief.

The Environment of Salvation. The word "environment" is used here in the usual dictionary sense, that is, as all the conditions, circumstances, or influences under which any person or thing lives or functions. It is the pattern of circumstances that are relevant to a thing's being what it is. It goes without saying that some aspects of the environment are more immediate and influential than others, but clearly some environment is indispensable to anything's being what it is. To abstract or iso-late anything from its natural environment is to get a distorted notion of what it really is. It is important for present purposes to point out that this definition seems to apply to all reality, from the subatomic environment to the environment of salvation for man.

Note first the application of the definition to the subatomic realm. There was a time when the prevailing notion of the atom was that it was the unchangeable building block of the universe. In other words, the atom was what it was regardless of the environment. But then the physicist split the atom and entered the strange world of electrons, protons, mesons, positrons, and so on. The most surprising aspect of the new subatomic world was that the subatomic entities could not be thought of as substance in the usual sense. They weren't hunks of anything but were patterns of active energy. Moreover, each one behaved as it did because of its relation to all the others. The revolutionary conclusion was that in the subatomic realms one had to acknowledge the primacy of process over structure, of function over substance. In other words, the subatomic entities were what they were because of their interdependent relationships with each other.

If the significance of this discovery were limited to the realms of subatomic physics, it would deserve no place in this study. But the fact is that more and more scholarly disciplines are discovering the significance of the primacy of function over substance for their own respective areas of study. The emergence of psychotherapy in modern medicine is a characteristic illustration. Whereas most physicians once looked upon symptoms in a narrowly organic sense, now most of them interpret the symptom in a broader functional way, especially in the more obvious cases of psychosomatic disorders. Many times the line between organic disease and psychosomatic malfunction is difficult to determine. The social scientists are discovering that the same principle often applies to the tribal, national, and international levels of human behavior.

The same notion of environment applies to human salvation. In characterizing the quest as clue to man in Section 2 above, we suggested that the most basic aspect of man is his "will to meaning." This means that what a man is today depends largely upon the way in which he has exercised his "will to meaning" in the past. In other words, the structure of his present life is largely dependent upon his sequence of previous environments —what he has eaten, decisions he has honored, friendships he has developed, and so on. Further, in the discussion of the secular mean between the extremes of otherworldliness and this-worldliness it was emphasized that man is no island in either space or time, that any analysis of "here" necessarily led to some notion of "there," and that any analysis of "now" led to some notion of "then." The relationship of this discussion to the notion of environment is obvious and intentional.

Three additional observations are relevant. First, if man is to enjoy an increasingly meaningful life he must control the appropriate environment accordingly. Man can be intelligent and learn from his experience. Nature is benevolent in yielding up her secrets to man's disciplined curiosity, and cooperative in responding dependably to his deliberate innovations. This basic rapport holds the potentiality for a long and happy relationship.

Secondly, and equally obvious, since all men are engaged in some form of goal-seeking, and since the numbers of men are increasing at a perilous rate, sooner or later the salvation endeavors must become cooperative or disastrous. Perhaps man is intelligent enough to realize that all of his fellowmen are teleological by nature, that all goals are not equally desirable or detrimental to the fulfilled life on earth, and that the means for discovering and establishing the most desirable goals is neither guns nor butter but rather imaginative negotiation and mutual flexibility.

Thirdly, there are aspects of the environment, both natural and human, that are resistant, obstructive, and destructive. They have puzzled philosophers and theologians for centuries. If one does not believe in an omni-God who is supposed to take man's cause as his own, or if one does not expect the world to be free from this so-called natural evil, there is no theological difficulty. The problem arises when one tries to square the omni-God with some of the horrible events in nature and history. But regardless of the way one attempts to deal with the problem of evil, the fact is that there are aspects of the environment which resist man's noblest efforts. These observations lead to another dimension in the process of secular salvation.

The Agent in Salvation. Many times individuals and groups are unable to obtain and maintain the necessary control of the environment to experience a meaningful life. At the individual level there are the many cases of psychosomatic disorders that require the assistance of a therapist. If we extend the environment to include the national and international scene, we have to admit that we are unable to prevent or control adequately some of the more tragic realities of our times: war, disease, famine, pollution, overpopulation, unemployment, prejudice, and superstition. The fact is that every man periodically finds himself in situations where he has insufficient control to assure himself of long-term secular salvation. Thus there is need for an agent who can be instrumental in fulfilling the individual and tribal quests for secular salvation.

Sometimes the role of the agent is independent of any conscious need, as in the many instances of cooperative endeavors that are mutually beneficial. The therapist-patient relationship is likely to be one-sided as far as intrinsic benefits are concerned. This seems to be the case in most instances involving acknowledged need. But in the mutually beneficial relationship one moves to a higher level of satisfaction where the role of the agent goes beyond the need. Each is an agent nonetheless. The next chapter will describe this relationship in more detail, but it should be noted in passing that the agent in every instance is a very special part of the environment.

Then, beyond all our individual and corporate efforts there is the place of "Grace."

Salvation as a Gift of "Grace." Salvation refers to that total life orientation which makes for the most and the best creative well-being. Much of the meaningful life is the result of diligent and disciplined effort, as the references to the environment and the agent have shown. But there is another dimension to salvation that seems strangely different and unrelated to effort—the sense of awe and wonder, of rapture and ecstasy, of *beholding* the Beyond in the midst of the familiar or sensing a Presence when one is alone by the sea under the stars. This aspect of salvation is so mysterious that even after coming and going it leaves us still unknowing. It is ineffable. One hesitates to speak of it for fear of appearing foolish, and yet, its personal power is such that one feels almost perfidious if he keeps an easy silence. Though reference to it is usually highly symbolic, a few verbal comments may be pardoned.

First, this aspect of salvation cannot be earned through effort. There are some desirable states of being that elude direct pursuit. Our common experience testifies all too clearly that some of the goals of life retreat from us the moment we pursue them. To try to fall asleep is to become distressingly conscious of your wakefulness. To attempt to forget either the dreadful or the tempting is to enslave yourself to its bondage. To pursue happiness directly is to court rare kinds of misery, and to try to make love to someone or to solicit urgently someone's love for you is invariably to mortgage your chances. Apparently it is accurate to say that "happiness is a goddess who forever eludes direct pursuit." This seems to be the case with this dimension of salvation. "He who would save his life will lose it." (Mark 8:35.)

Secondly, an attitude of commitment is essential. This means entrusting oneself to the custody of another. After one has studied the environment of salvation and ascertained both the benefits and the limits of effort, a final act is essential, that of abandoning oneself to the creative process.[19] This is "casting your bread upon the waters," making an investment with no assurance of a return. Commitment is a vulnerable exposure in trust.

Thirdly, one must acknowledge the fact of both risk and luck. To define commitment as a vulnerable exposure in trust is to indicate clearly that a real risk is involved. But it is a risk that must be taken. If one is to know the thrill of high adventure, he must brave the dangers of ocean, forest, and mountain. Luck also seems to be a part of the total pattern of salvation. There is no convincing evidence that nature is concerned with the goals of the individual man. There are many instances in which virtue is not appropriately rewarded nor wickedness appropriately disciplined. As man's knowledge increases he will be able to eliminate much of the risk and improve the chances for good fortune, but for the present we must acknowledge both risk and luck, and that some are luckier than others.

Hence, one must conclude that this aspect of salvation is a gift of "Grace." It is a gift because it cannot be earned through effort, wooed through flattery, or won through trickery. It seems to come as a kind of surprise while the attention is directed elsewhere. It is an "unbirthday present." But can one speak of a gift without assuming a giver? And further, is there any clue to the giver in the nature of the gift? Often by the time one has discovered the gift, the giver has gone; and yet, the giver is strangely present in the gift. Now the mystery of "Grace" begins to appear.

"Grace" refers to that vast pool of potentiality from which streams of blessings flow. It is hidden. It is like a cool, clear, crystal fountain of water, bubbling from the earth, with its source unknown. To keep it fresh and flowing it must be freely used to wash one's thirst and cool one's flesh. Selfishly to seal it in some flask is to rub its sparkle out and rob it of its power. Like love, to keep it one must give it away without record or expectant recompense. It is a mysterious and ineffable aspect of the environment. And yet, the fact is, Grace *is;* and man is saved by Grace.

CHAPTER III

The Secular Christ
as Savior

AT first glance the title of this chapter does not make sense. If one were to omit the word "secular" and speak simply of "the Christ as Savior," the title would have an old familiar ring. To introduce the word "secular" is to make confusion because it refers to this earth and this world while the saving work of "Christ" in traditional Christianity has to do primarily with an otherworld. This chapter will attempt to show that the basic confusion is in the traditional interpretation of the word "Christ" and that when it is used accurately it makes good sense to speak of the secular christ as savior. This effort begins with a brief definition of the term and then continues with a more detailed discussion of the relationship between Jesus and the christs.

1. The Meaning of "Christ"

The preceding chapter suggested that modern man adapt the notion of salvation to secular usage. This chapter will make the same recommendation with the term "christ," acknowledging that the usage will seem strange to Christians at first. Before the end of this discussion it will be evident why this adaptation is being made.

Christ as the Agent in Salvation. It was argued earlier that the quest for secular salvation is the most fundamental clue to man, both individually and socially, that salvation does not happen in a vacuum but usually requires an environment that is ordered creatively, and that many people often need assistance in the salvation process because of a resistant or obstructive element in their environment. In this chapter and throughout the book the word "christ" will mean "the agent in salvation." No single theme is more central to the study as a whole. It will involve revolutionary changes from the current orthodox way of thinking. To define and defend this usage, this study will refer to a number of scholarly studies, to the scriptures of the Judeo-Christian tradition, and to the scriptures of other world religions. In each case the evidence will support this more general and less parochial point of view over the traditional views of the past and present. Hence, the word "christ" will be used to refer to any human agent in the process of salvation.

Since "Christ" is often used as a personal name, as synonymous with Jesus or Jesus Christ, we need to make some important distinctions to avoid serious ambiguity.

The Distinction Between Jesus and Christ. "Jesus" and "christ" are not synonymous and should not be used as if they were. "Jesus" is a masculine name that was commonly used in the earliest Judeo-Christian tradition. The Hebrew form was Joshua, meaning "he whose salvation is Yahweh."[20] It is still a common name in some Latin American countries. In this study it will refer to a specific man from Nazareth in Galilee nearly two thousand years ago.

The word "christ" is much more complex and problematic. It comes from the Greek form, *christos,* which serves as the equivalent of the Hebrew word for the Lord's "anointed." Since Biblical literature refers to a number of different people as the Lord's anointed, we will argue here that it is a general term which refers to a role or function rather than a personal name for a specific man. Just as we ought not confuse the function or office of, say, the President of the United States with a particular man who has filled or currently fills that office, so also we must not confuse the man Jesus with the christ function. To be sure, the office influences the man and the man influences the notion of the office, but they are not identical either in the structure of government or in the structure of salvation. To clarify and defend this point of view we need to take a brief look at some of the christological titles and functions that are relevant to traditional Christianity. In doing so we will make more clear the necessary distinction between Jesus and christ.

2. THE CHRISTS BEFORE JESUS

Obviously, to speak of "the christs before Jesus" is to use language that requires clarification. Such a title presupposes at least two relevant points. One is the historical distinction between Jesus and christ as suggested above. Another is that the plural form "christs" can be discussed in some meaningful way without specific reference to Jesus. Having emphasized the distinction between the man, Jesus, and the role or function, christ, we can now suggest that the term "christs" may refer *either* to multiple interpretations of a messianic role or function as suggested by the many different christological *titles or* to historical or imaginary *persons* who have been thought to have filled the designated role or function. Each of these alternatives is important to the present chapter. The former will be considered here while the latter will be examined in Section 5 below.

The Many Relevant Christological Titles. Messianic expectation has played a basic role in the development of the Judeo-Christian tradition. The religion of the Old Testament is salvation-oriented around such notions as the Promised Land, the Day of Yahweh, and the New Zion. The coming of a messiah who would carry out the ordained role in salvation is central to an accurate understanding of Old Testament religion.[21] The Intertestamental period, that is, the two or three centuries prior to the birth of Jesus, reflects the continuing intensity of the messianic expectancy. Apparently the community of the Dead Sea Scrolls expected *two* messiahs, one kingly and one priestly. The New Testament tries to convince the reader that the messianic expectations have been fulfilled in Jesus of Nazareth.

But the important fact that must not escape our notice is that there was a great variety of interpretations of the one or ones expected. Indeed, there seems never to have been a time when all people agreed on the nature or function of the messiahs expected. This can be illustrated by identifying some of the many relevant christological titles that were a part of the evolving tradition.

New Testament christology utilizes three earlier traditions: Palestinian Judaism, Hellenistic Judaism, and Hellenistic Gentilism. Each of these three traditions developed various christological notions that are fundamental in understanding the titles applied to Jesus of Nazareth. For example, in Palestinian Judaism there were such titles as Messiah, Son of God, Son of Man, Son of David, High Priest, Servant of the Lord, Eschatological Prophet, Word, Lord, and Savior. Hellenistic Judaism utilized such notions as Christos, Kyrios, Wisdom, and Logos. Included in Hellenistic Gentilism are the "Imperial Cultus," the "Mystery Religions," the "Gnostic Redeemer Myth," and the "Divine Man."[22] From these lists one can see the great variety of titles that were a part of the religious expectancy of the late Old Testament and Intertestamental times.

Another complicating factor in New Testament christology is the uncertainty of interpretation of the titles. The literature of the Old Testament developed over a period of more than a thousand years. During that time there were several great empires governing the territory from time to time, each leaving its impact upon the culture that followed. These influences naturally found their way into the interpretations of the christological titles. The results are obvious. Not only are there many different titles; there are many interpretations of the many titles. Taken in abstraction the titles are often confusing or even contradictory. To make sense of them one must see them in terms of their cultural context. For example, in the Hellenistic world the title "Lord" could refer either to a master or to an emperor. If it referred to the emperor, it could have either a profane usage signifying political patriotism or a religious intent as in the case of emperor worship. In the Hebrew world it could refer either to another man or to God. In the cases of religious usage where deity was acknowledged, the interpretations of the Greek and the Hebrew were very different indeed. When the cultural context is unknown, discussion of any title is largely speculative.

The Common Aspect of the Titles. Though it is accurate to suggest that each of the titles has some peculiar function that separates it from all the others, careful study of the titles reveals that they all have something in common. In some way each and every one serves as an agent in salvation. When properly incarnated, each and every one adds a dimension of meaning or fulfillment to the common life. Though the language and the cultural context may vary noticeably, each and every one depicts within a larger framework the kind of creative development that has been defined here as the process of salvation. These details help to clarify the sense in which we are using the term "christs" and further, what we mean by *"christ-ological."* Hence, to repeat, "christ" refers to any human agent in the process of salvation.

3. THE CHRISTS FOR JESUS

Because the times of Jesus were christologically oriented, and because traditional Christianity has looked upon Jesus as the ultimate authority in religion and morality, it is both appropriate and necessary at this point to ponder the relevance and meaning of the various christological titles for Jesus himself. Just as one must understand the titles in terms of their cultural context, so one must understand Jesus in terms of his time and place. It is generally agreed that messianic expectancy was primal in his day. Hence, we naturally wonder about his attitude toward the various christological categories.

From the outset our pondering encounters several obstacles. One is the strangeness of the language. Christians have not been taught to think in this way. The topic of this section, "The Christs for Jesus," will sound weird and puzzling, probably because of a failure to appreciate the necessary distinction between Jesus and christ. Once the importance of that distinction is clear, the language here will seem normal and helpful.

Another, and far more formidable obstacle, has to do with our sources of information. Since we have no record of any writings of Jesus, we are entirely at the mercy of the secondary sources—the New Testament and scholarly commentaries. The long and crucial debate over the historical reliability of the Synoptic Gospels continues among New Testament scholars today. In the next section we will identify some of the causes of the debate and give reasons why it should be taken seriously, but for the moment we are going to assume that the New Testament sources, especially the Synoptic Gospels, are reliable for present purposes. Without this preliminary (and questionable) assumption discussion of this topic would be impossible.

A third obstacle, which may well be insurmountable, is the fact that our Biblical information on Jesus' attitude toward the various christological categories is set entirely within the framework of his own relationship to them. At best it is difficult to know the self-consciousness of anyone, and whether or not the New Testament sources permit this kind of analysis of the self-consciousness of Jesus continues to be a subject for enthusiastic debate. But since part of the teachings of Jesus deals with his understanding of his person and ministry, and since the teachings of Jesus have been fundamental to traditional Christianity, and since this particular topic—that is, "The Christs for Jesus"—is important to this study, we pursue it in spite of the obstacles.

The Christological Claims by Jesus. There are two passages in which Jesus claims outright to be the Christ. First, and more important, is his direct and affirmative reply to the question of Caiaphas, the high priest: "Are you the Christ, the Son of the Blessed?" And Jesus said, "I am; and you will see the Son of man sitting at the right hand of Power" (Mark 14:61–62). A second reference comes from the Gospel of John. A woman of Samaria said to Jesus, "I know that Messiah is coming (he who is called Christ); when he comes, he will show us all things." And Jesus said to her, "I who speak to you am he." (John 4:25–26.)

There are a few passages where the claims are indirect or by implication only. For example, when Jesus asked the disciples "Who do men say that I am?" and Peter replied, "You are the Christ," Jesus accepted the "great confession" and charged the disciples to tell no one about him (Mark 8:27–30). Another example is the so-called triumphal entry into Jerusalem which is believed to have messianic implications (Mark 11:1–11). Or further, the "But I say to you" passages from the Sermon on the Mount could be interpreted as messianic by implication (Matt. 5:21–48).

The christological title that Jesus utilizes in his understanding of his person and ministry is "Son of man." In his reply to Caiaphas he uses the title as in some sense synonymous with "Christ," but in the Synoptic Gospels as a whole, he clearly prefers the title "Son of man." The "I am" passages in the Gospel of John, for example, "I am the bread of life" (ch 6:35); "I am the light of the world" (ch 8:12); "I am the way, the truth, and the life" (ch 14:6)—these and other passages clearly suggest that Jesus understood his person and ministry in a special way.

But just as there is evidence that Jesus interpreted his life and ministry in a christological way, so also there is evidence that he was uncertain about messianic election.

The Christological Doubts of Jesus. Since the primary purpose of the New Testament is to persuade the reader that Jesus is the Christ of Jewish expectation, it is far easier to argue his christological claims than his christological uncertainties. But several passages need to be cited in this connection. When the rich young ruler came to Jesus and addressed him as "Good Teacher," Jesus retorted, "Why do you call me good? No one is good but God alone" (Mark 10:17–18). Although this is not an outright denial of a christological function, it does mark a clear distinction between God and Jesus as far as goodness is concerned. (Yet the "I am" passages from the Gospel of John suggest that Jesus is far more than good, and clearly imply a special relationship with God.)

Two additional references seem to suggest that Jesus was uncertain or that he might be trying to make up his mind about his christological purposes. One comes in a question he directed to his disciples after a brief period of intensive missionary activity, "Who do men say that I am?" (Mark 8:27). Though the impression is that he was seeking a reaction from the disciples to guide his future plans, it is conceivable that he might have been seeking reassurance in his own mind. Though Peter acknowledges him as "the Christ," in Jesus' response to Peter he referred to himself as the "Son of man" (Mark 8:31 ff.). Secondly, when John the Baptist sent a delegation from prison to Jesus inquiring, "Are you he who is to come, or shall we look for another?" Jesus neither affirms nor denies but rather replies in such a way that John has to decide for himself (Matt. 11:3–6). If Jesus had been certain at that point and knew what was coming, why did he not say so and permit John the Baptist to die in peace?

Obviously these few passages do not constitute an extensive argument that Jesus denied any messianic function. At best they imply that insofar as the messianic self-consciousness of Jesus can be known, it was a developing awareness. Far more important is the discovery of the central theme in the teachings of Jesus which would serve as a better clue to his understanding of himself and his times.

The Primacy of the Kingdom of God. Careful study of the Synoptic Gospels shows that the teachings of Jesus are far more concerned with the Kingdom of God than with his own messianic election or function. His primary concern seems to be that the Kingdom of God is at hand and that people should make right before God their ways of living in order that they might participate in the joys and blessings of that imminent event. As a new Jeremiah, he seems concerned primarily with a new covenant that involves a new notion of righteousness. Moreover, the higher righteousness that is eloquently outlined in the Sermon on the Mount seems to be both reliable and challenging, not because of the office of the preacher as much as because of the content of the sermon. Jesus seems far more occupied with a man's relations with his fellowmen than he is with his own christological function. This is so generally agreed to be the case in the Synoptic Gospels that the point need not be labored longer. The relationship of the messianic office to the coming of the Kingdom of God seems to be of secondary importance in the Synoptic Gospels.

Conclusion: Jesus Uncertain About Christ. On the one hand, there is Biblical evidence that Jesus made christological claims in terms of both "Christ" and "Son of man," although these titles cannot be interpreted as synonymous in either late Old Testament times or in the Intertestamental period. On the other hand, there is Biblical evidence that Jesus might himself have been uncertain about his christological role. The result is that New Testament scholars disagree on whether or not Jesus claimed to be the messiah of Jewish expectation.[23] If any conclusion can be drawn from all of this, it surely must be that we simply do not know with any kind of certainty what Jesus considered his relationship to the christological titles to be. The Synoptic Gospels seem to indicate that Jesus was more concerned about the Kingdom of God than he was with his messianic function. The proclaim*er* seems to have become the proclaim*ed*. The religion *of* Jesus seems to have become a religion *about* Jesus. The notions of "christ" and "christian" as developed in this study may help, hopefully, to clarify these issues.

4. JESUS, A CHRIST

As indicated earlier, there has been a lot of unnecessary confusion in Christian literature and theology because of the failure to distinguish adequately between Jesus and christ. This section will attempt a more detailed description of the distinction and a further discussion of the relationship.

Jesus and the Historical Sources. Traditional Christianity has been largely Christ-centered. The very name of this world religion reflects this fact in that the key word is "Christ" (*Christ*ianity) and not "God." Further, in its theology and in its worship Christ has been focal. But it almost goes without saying that "Christ" here really means "Jesus." As suggested earlier, the New Testament accounts reflect a transition from a religion *of* Jesus to a religion *about* Jesus; the proclaim*er* becomes the Proclaim*ed*. For all intents and purposes, Jesus becomes the God of traditional Christianity. His precept is its truth, his exemplary action its practical guide.

In a religion that is oriented around a man it is only natural to seek the greatest amount of knowledge about him. If something is true because he said it, we naturally ask, "What did he say?" If something is right because he did it, we naturally inquire, "What did he do?" Since the only source for answering these questions is the New Testament, traditional Christianity, especially Protestantism, has been largely New Testament oriented.

But to turn to the New Testament for the essentials of the life and teachings of Jesus is to encounter serious difficulties. The Synoptic Gospels disagree on such fundamentals as the genealogy of Jesus, the flight into Egypt, the one addressed by God at the baptism of Jesus, the order of the temptations of Jesus, and the Lord's Prayer.[24] If one includes the Gospel of John in the research, the contradictions are even more evident. There are differences in the chronology of Jesus' ministry and the length of the ministry. The scene of the center of activity is shifted from Galilee to Judea and Jerusalem; the parables and the short prophetic utterances of the Synoptics become long philosophical discourses in John; the central themes are different, and most evident and most important for our present purposes is the difference in the attitude of Jesus toward himself and his ministry. In the Synoptics he is often obviously and deliberately hesitant in any messianic claims, whereas in the Gospel of John he proudly acknowledges that he is the Christ and performs miracles to prove it. Since our information is limited to the fragmentary and inconsistent accounts in the Gospels, we have to acknowledge a real problem in attempting to know the historical Jesus.

To help solve the problem of the sources some New Testament scholars have developed the thesis that we should think of the gospel records as "kerygma" rather than as "history." The theory is that the gospel accounts were never intended to be interpreted as objective factual accounts of events, places, and dates. Rather, they were proclamations about the significance of Jesus as the Messiah. "Kerygma" has become a technical term with a double meaning; it may refer either to the *content* of the proclamation or to the *act* of proclaiming itself. The scholars are not agreed on this as it is easy to see. The sermons of the earliest disciples submit easily to the kerygma hypothesis, but what about the passages referring to events of a certain place and time: the birth in Bethlehem, the flight into Egypt, the time and place of the crucifixion or resurrection, and so on?

To interpret all the gospel records as kerygma rather than history is to face several serious consequences. First, it leaves us with no reliable evidence for an actual historical Jesus. To be sure, it minimizes the discrepancies in the Gospels, but one is left to decide whether or not the price is too great. The enthusiastic disagreement among the scholars extends from the one extreme of denying that there ever was a historical Jesus to the other extreme of insisting that the Gospels are reliable historical records. A second important consequence in the shift from history to kerygma involves the notion of shifting authority. For traditional Christianity, the historical Jesus has been the authority in both precept and example. What he said was true because *he* said it; what he did was exemplary because *he* did it. It is one thing to respect and honor a precept because of the authority of the teacher; it is quite another thing to honor what the student may proclaim to be true about the teacher. In "history" we presumably have the authority of the teacher (or Jesus in this case) while in "kerygma" we have only the authority of the student (or disciple in this case). To the extent that one shifts from the Jesus of history to the Christ of kerygma, to that extent the authority of Jesus is lost. A third and similar kind of consequence involves the problem of continuity between Jesus and Paul. The content of the Synoptic Gospels suggests that Jesus believed the end of the age was at hand, that the Kingdom of God was imminent and, perhaps, that a divine mediator would be instrumental in establishing this sequence of events. The content of Paul's preaching tends to assert that the event has happened—past, not future—in the life, death, and resurrection of Jesus as the Christ. The puzzling question is: Did Jesus preach one gospel while Paul and the early church preached another? It appears, as suggested earlier, that the religion *of* Jesus has actually become a religion *about* Jesus.

Fortunately, it is not essential to our thesis that all these issues be resolved. We have admitted that there are equally cogent conflicting arguments with conclusions which disagree. For clarity we acknowledge the unsolved problems of history and kerygma, and the uncertainty of the content of the teaching or preaching of Jesus; but this study sides with those who believe that something can be known about the man behind the myth, though specific biographical detail is inaccessible. Beyond this, there is a way out of the dilemma through a more practicable understanding of the notion of "christ."

Jesus as a Christ. Having indicated clearly what is meant by both Jesus and Christ, we can now conclude, first, that Jesus obviously was *a* christ for some people in the sense in which this study is using the term. He served as a significant agent in salvation for a number of people, whether in exorcising demons, healings of various other kinds, in giving general advice or providing profound fulfillment for life. Peter's great confession proclaims this, at least for Peter (Mark 8:29), as does the story of Mary Magdalene for Mary (John 8:1–11). The kerygma hypothesis supports this point of view.

On the other hand, secondly, one must acknowledge that Jesus was not a christ for all. Some of his teachings and actions not only did not save, say, the Sanhedrin or the representatives of the Roman Government, but were actually a hindrance to effective and harmonious legislation. The money changers in the Temple must have found him an intolerable nuisance at best. Traditional Christianity would have us believe that Jesus was a Christ for all whether they recognized it or not. Such a point of view presupposes either the old mythological or a substance christology which advocates that Jesus did what he did because he was who he was. This study suggests a functional approach which says that Jesus was who he was because he did what he did. In any case, the fact is that many of Jesus' contemporaries did not find him to be an agent of salvation. To charge them with either insincerity or sin is parochial foolishness. The incontrovertible conclusion is that Jesus was a christ for some and not a christ for others.

Jesus as the *Christ.* Several factors may have been involved in leading the disciples, Paul, and the early church into addressing Jesus as *the* Christ. First, and probably most important, is the empirical impact that he had on some of the people he met. Those who were saved through his thought or deed were at a loss to give him a name. For them his influence was so transforming that he shattered the significance of the differences of the various christological titles. To them he was *the* High Priest, *the* Logos, *the* Son of Man, *the* Son of God, *the* Christ —all in one. An experience of salvation can be so overwhelming as to reduce to absurdity the distinction between one christological title and another. Moreover, to the common ones who heard him gladly the messianic differences between one name or another would probably have been minimal. On being healed a lame man does not philosophize; he dances in ecstasy.

In addition to this important empirical factor, there may have been aspects of a more subtle kind. For example, there may well have been an intense natural desire for a common corporate Messiah, especially after the tensions of opposition began to appear. External hostility has a tendency to unify the tribe and there is reason to believe that this was the case with the earliest Christians. Or a later mythology may have called for a singular Christ figure. The mythology of Jesus' time involved multiple notions as we have seen in the sect of the Dead Sea Scrolls. Or a more technical transition may also have been relevant. Oscar Cullmann has pointed out that in the Hellenistic usage of the title *Kyrios,* there was a transition from "a lord" or "my Lord" to "the Lord." In the Christian community there seems to have been a corresponding transition in the use of the Aramaic equivalent, *mar,* after the resurrection.[25] In any case, the Christian Church referred to Jesus as *the* Christ.

Whatever the reasons may have been which led to Jesus' being called the Christ, there are several obvious reasons why we cannot continue to refer to Jesus as "the Christ" today. First, such a reference implies that there is only one christ when actually there can be many. We have seen the multiplicity illustrated in the case of the christological titles. Not only are there a number of different roles; the functions are so diverse as to make uniformity or singularity impossible. For example, how does one relate the interpretation of the "Son of Man" or the "Logos" as *preexistent* with the "Messiah" as Davidic? Or how does one relate the interpretation of the "Son of Man" as heavenly or the *Kyrios* as divine with the "Son of David" as human (in the framework of early Palestinian Christianity)? Cullmann tries to apply all the titles to Jesus by showing that some refer to "the earthly work of Jesus," some to the "future work," some to the "present work," and some to the "pre-existence of Jesus." That Jesus could have been the incarnation of all of them is dubious at best.

Secondly, Jesus cannot be called *the* christ because there are different christs for different salvation situations. Just as there were many different notions of salvation in Jesus' time, so also there are many different notions of salvation today. The quest for salvation is common to all of us, but the ideas of the fulfillment of the quest are numerous and varied. Not only do different people have differing notions of salvation, even the same person changes his attitude from time to time. Since "christ" has been defined as a "human agent in salvation," we must allow for the same variety of christs as there are notions of salvation. Hence, to speak of *the* christ is to revert to a primitive mythology or a substance christology that has long since passed, or it is to assume a single pattern of expectation of salvation that simply does not exist today. It is just as foolish as speaking of *the* best move in chess. This study acknowledges that Jesus was *a* christ for some but insists that the notion of Jesus as *the* christ is long since obsolete and detrimental. After all, there are many sincere and enlightened people today for whom Jesus is not a christ. There are christs besides Jesus.

5. THE CHRISTS BESIDES JESUS

In the section "The Christs Before Jesus" we were concerned with the various christological titles that have played a role in the development of the Judeo-Christian tradition. In this section we are interested in identifying some significant historical persons who have been proclaimed as "christs." This can be done by focusing upon the christs in the Old Testament, the christs in other world religions, and some of the contemporary christs.

The Christs in the Old Testament. Most Christians are so accustomed to associating the term "christ" with the New Testament that they would be inclined to deny that there are any christs in the Old Testament. Careful reading of Old Testament literature indicates clearly that messianic speculation *and* proclamation began quite early in the development of Judaism. To illustrate, Isaiah predicted the imminent birth of a prince of peace in passages now very familiar: "Behold, a young woman shall conceive and bear a son" (Isa. 7:14). But Deutero-Isaiah went farther and proclaimed Cyrus of Persia as the "anointed" of the Lord, who was given the great commission "to subdue nations before him, and ungird the loins of kings, to open doors before him that gates may not be closed" (Isa. 45:1 ff.). Haggai and Zechariah both regarded Zerubbabel as especially anointed of the Lord, that is, as a christ (Hag. 2:23 and Zech. 4:6–10). Hence, it is accurate to conclude that there were not only *christo*logical speculations and predictions in Old Testament literature from time to time, but there were proclamations (kerygma?) as well. In the sense in which we have defined the term, Moses, Joshua, some of the Judges, David and some of the other kings, and some of the prophets have fulfilled christian functions.

The Christs in Other World Religions. The role of a christ is not unique to Judaism or Christianity. According to the *Gita*, in Hinduism salvation comes through Krishna. In Buddhism salvation comes through one or more of the many Buddhas. If we use the term "christ" as "an agent in salvation," it can be said without hesitation or qualification that Moses was a christ in Judaism, Zoroaster in Zoroastrianism, Lao-tzu in Taoism, Confucius in Confucianism, Mahavira in Jainism, Muhammad in Islam, and Nanak in Sikhism. With qualification a good deal more could be said about the soteriological benefits of these founders of great world religions. But this brief discussion is sufficient to demonstrate the christ function in other world religions.[26]

The Contemporary Christs. With the exception of Nanak and Muhammad all the christs of the world religions mentioned above were born five centuries or more before Jesus. This might suggest to the casual observer that the advent day of the christs is long since past. Far from it. A study of the history of religion in America will show that there are at least two more recent christs, each with a formal following: Joseph Smith for the Mormons and Mary Baker Eddy for the Christian Scientists. Neither of these religions would suggest that their founders are to be compared with Jesus in religious significance, but, by our legitimate definition, each has been and continues to be a christ to the members of these religious sects.

There are other contemporary christs who have their followers but who are not so formalized in temple and scripture. Such names as "Mahatma" Gandhi, Albert Schweitzer, John F. Kennedy, Martin Luther King, and Mao Tse-tung—to cite only a few—would be nominated from various significant sectors of our world and culture. The fact is that each of these, and others who could be mentioned, has been a christ for many people. This realization leads directly to the next topic.

6. Christ Without Jesus

A further important aspect of the distinction between Jesus and christ can be seen in a brief discussion of "christ without Jesus." Just as there are many who have "Jesus without Christ," that is, they accept Jesus as a prophet or a teacher but not as a Christ, so also there are many who have a "christ without Jesus" as seen in the discussions of "the christs before Jesus" and "the christs besides Jesus." In the first chapter we suggested that there could be a "christology without Jesus." Now we need to make a few summarizing comments directed specifically to that theme.

The Christian Agency and a Christ as Agent. We have frequently referred to the christ notion as the agent in salvation. When we recall that the quest for salvation is both universal and eternal, and when we realize as well that the need for an agent seems forever to recur, we discover a pattern or structure within the process of salvation that might well utilize the notion of "agency." In referring to the christ *office* we have introduced the notion already. At this point we need to clarify the relation between the agency and the agent. In one sense they are separate; in another they are identical.

One can interpret the agency and the agent as separate when one looks at them objectively as identifiable parts of a larger system or world view. In this sense one can define what he means by salvation and analyze its structure and function. For the moment he is not involved in it but viewing it from a distance, so to speak. To do this is to discover some characteristic features, some of which were identified in the second chapter. In this way of thinking one can distinguish between the agency and the agent, the office and the man.

In another sense, however, the distinction loses its significance. In subjective or empirical experience the two can become identical if only momentarily. When one is actually involved in a salvation experience which clearly utilizes an agent, at that moment the christ assumes a face and a name. This seems to be the key to understanding the mystery of *incarnation*, when something profound and eternal becomes real and momentary in life, "the Word made flesh." The christ office or agency seems abstract until someone fills the role. The agent can change things; indeed, the agent can change things so profoundly that one will reorient his whole life. Jesus seems to have had exactly that effect upon a number of people he met, whose lives were so changed that he abolished the significance of the differences in the christological categories. Small wonder that for those people Jesus was *the* Christ. The office and the man became indistinguishable.

But another aspect of the relation between agency and agent must be acknowledged.

The Agency Abides; the Agent Passes. As defined above, the christian agency is obviously more important and enduring than the agent or man who fills it. The office has been shown to have been, and still to be, operating in other cultures and world religions. It serves as a part of the "clue" to man, age after age. Were one to compare the scope of each, that is, of agency and agent, as one could do in discussing either "Jesus without christ" or "christ without Jesus," he would have to conclude from the evidence that the christ office or function appears and abides while the acknowledged agent appears and passes. Moreover, this is as it should be. Some christian relations should be temporary. For example, in the event of illness one needs a physician and in his capacity as physician he may well be an agent of salvation, a christ. But if he performs his office effectively, the need for the agent will pass. The same is true in the parent-child relation. Part of the task of a responsible parent is to rear the child so that the need for the parent *as parent* passes. Thus, in some instances a passing agent testifies to strength rather than weakness.

A peculiar problem arises for traditional Christians when the agency is christ and the agent is Jesus. They have always assumed that the need for either a physician or a parent should pass. They expect the presidents to change from election to election. But they have been taught that there is an eternal relevance in Jesus of Nazareth that defies both cultural context or geographical location. Christians are willing to acknowledge that Moses and Jeremiah were men of their own times and that to understand the religion of either of them we need to understand them in terms of their times. Furthermore, Christians are willing to admit that Jeremiah's new covenant replaced the obsolete covenant of Moses (especially the second commandment) and that Jesus' New Testament (Covenant) replaced the Old Testament. And yet, in spite of the fact that two thousand years of historical evolution have taken place since the time of Jesus, and that our world has much less in common with his than did his world with that of Jeremiah, many traditional Christians will be horrified by the suggestion that the relevance of Jesus to the contemporary world has largely passed. In an all-out effort to establish the eternal relevance of Jesus some adept textualists will lift selected precepts from the New Testament record and argue that they reflect the real Jesus and that they are both relevant and reliable forever. The adept Muslim, Buddhist, or Hindu could do the same thing for Muhammad, Amitabha, or Krishna. The honest Christian must be willing to face the possibility that the day of the relevance of Jesus is passing.

Because of the danger of being misunderstood, we need to emphasize that this does not mean that Jesus is not a christ in any sense. Nor does it mean that all Christians must abandon all his teachings or his example. It does mean that traditional Christians will have to stop speaking of Jesus as if he were the only legitimate christ, *or* acknowledge that their confession is no more than a personal preference. This does not mean, further, that our christ is Jesus-*less*; rather, it is Jesus-*plus*. It takes from the tradition all that is relevant and adds to it much that goes beyond the tradition. Moreover, for many of us the key to the christ notion is in the plus. In this sense "christ without Jesus" is a plea as well as a verdict. It is not a negative and reductive notion but rather a positive and creative notion that is essential for our times. We are indebted to Prof. Henry J. Cadbury for rightly emphasizing "the peril of modernizing Jesus."[27] There may be an even greater peril for us in *not* modernizing the christ notion, that is, in failing to see its historic relevance in our own times.

Buddha Without Gautama. This point is added for emphasis, to illustrate that we should apply the notion of "christ without Jesus" to the other world religions as well as to Christianity and Judaism. Contemporary religion, and religions, must learn from Alfred North Whitehead and others that it will not fulfill its potential until it assumes a responsible attitude toward change, as has science.[28] Perhaps the day of "Gautama" is passing or is past? With "the Buddha" it is a different story. There will never be another Gandhi, but we hope there will be many another "Mahatma."

7. Secular Salvation and Secular Christ

This concluding general section of the chapter must include a brief discussion of several topics which will tie together some earlier remarks, show the relation between secular salvation and the secular christs, and serve as transition to the next chapter.

Salvation as Initial and Christ as Derivative. Early in the second chapter we indicated that the notion of salvation would be our point of departure and that all other theological notions would be subordinated to it and derive their meaning accordingly. It should be clear at this point why the christology developed in this chapter is dependent upon the prerequisite soteriology detailed in Chapter II. Hence, if anyone were to ask, "Does Jesus save because he is the Christ, or is Jesus a christ because he saves?" the answer clearly would be the latter. The notion of christ derives its meaning entirely in terms of the conception of salvation. To reverse the order and subordinate the notion of salvation to the notion of christ, especially as Christ is interpreted in traditional Christianity, is to limit it either to a Jesus ethic or to an apocalyptic-eschatological-mythological theology. Neither of these alternatives is desirable, since each is difficult to define and, insofar as it is definable, it seems irrelevant to our contemporary world. But with soteriology as initial and christology as derivative one seems not only to escape these limitations but also to provide an argument that is far more challenging in the contemporary world.

Christ as Secular and Sacred. In discussing the quest for salvation as secular we defined the term to refer not only to a this-worldly orientation rather than an otherworldly one but also to apply to the contemporary world rather than to the world of the ancient past. Exactly the same meaning is intended when we refer to christ as secular. In "christ without Jesus" we argued that we need to eliminate anything which prevents the christ agency from functioning effectively in the contemporary world. Hence, to discuss christ as secular is to review the notion of keeping the christ function current or modern so that it is seen to be relevant to our own life and time. To speak of christ as secular is to acknowledge both our need for and our participation in the current christ relationships. This is not alien to the notion of christ as sacred.

When the words "secular" and "sacred" are used in close conjunction, one has the immediate impression of contrast. Secular is thought to refer to the nonreligious or nonchurch, whereas sacred is presumed to refer to the specifically religious or ecclesiastical. No such contrasting distinction is intended here. Just as the secular may refer to the here and now so also the sacred may refer to the here and now, or at least be manifested in the here and now. Hence, our primary relation between them is complementary or conjunctive rather than disjunctive.

The word "sacred" is used here in its usual way, referring to something "exclusively appropriated to some person or to some special purpose,"[29] to that which is touched with mystery and awe, and hence not fully understood. Mircea Eliade has attempted to define the sacred by contrasting it with the profane. The profane refers to the natural desacralized world; the sacred refers to that which manifests itself in a hierophany, the "act of manifestation." Any object, group of objects, or even the entire cosmos may serve as a medium for a hierophany. But in this function the object represents a paradox. To the detached observer the object is what it is, participating in its realm of objects; but for those to whom the object reveals itself as sacred, "its immediate reality is transmuted into a supernatural reality."[30]

We have seen that one aspect of salvation involves experiences that are intense and momentary, awe-inspiring and overwhelming—encounters with a reality that is mysterious and fascinating. As an agent in salvation a christ is special environment and as special environment is instrumental in a hierophany. As agent it illustrates the paradox Eliade has identified. It participates in the here and now and is fully secular in that sense, but as agent it transmutes itself, and the here and now, to effect a total experience including mystery and wonder, and thus participates in the sacred as well. The agency of a christ can be compared with the mysterious function of a symbol in the thought of Paul Tillich—it realizes, reveals, and relates new dimensions of reality.[31] Hence, our designation of christ as sacred.

The Human Christ and the Nonhuman Agent. In contrasting the sacred and the profane we see that any object or combination of objects can mediate the sacred in a hierophany or theophany. In the familiar language of secular christianity this means that any object, person, or event can serve as an agent in salvation. This is especially evident in the aspects of salvation that are momentary and intense. Who of us has not beheld the full moon on the forest or the flowing tide, the mockingbird at dawn and the first star at dusk, a storm at sea or lightning in the mountains, or a setting sun on one side and a full rainbow on the other? All mystifying, all full of wonder! The list could fill pages, utilizing the nonhuman agent rather than the human. Acknowledging that anything in particular or the cosmos as a whole may serve as a medium for the Beyond, we limit the term "christ" to refer to the human agent in salvation and leave to a later chapter the nomenclature and discussion of the role of the nonhuman: nature, history, and God.

Christ as Claimed and Proclaimed. As we have defined the term, no one is a christ until the salvation benefits are acknowledged. To the extent that one can serve as an agent in his own salvation, to that extent he can claim to be a christ to himself; but beyond that, no one can claim to be a christ except on the previous proclamation of another. The meaning can be clarified with a few illustrations. No man can announce himself as a husband until some lady has accepted him as such in marriage. "Husband" and "wife" are relational terms which bride and groom announce of the other respectively. No man claims the presidency; rather, the citizens proclaim and inaugurate a man to become president temporarily. A prince can become a king because of his genealogy, but he cannot remain royal without the appropriate honor and homage of his kingdom. Like "husband," "president," or "king," "christ" is a relational term. Citizenship, blood type, or genealogy have nothing to do with it, but proclamation (kerygma) is a prerequisite.

The contrast between this point of view and that of traditional Christianity is evident. This is a functional christology, and anyone can be a christ who fills the christ function as defined. Traditional Christianity subscribes to a substantial christology which suggests that Jesus is the Christ because of who he is. He is the Christ because of genealogy, because he is a son of David's line, or Son of the Virgin Mary, or Son of God by being of the same substance as the Father, or by being the Son by adoption. In other words, in traditional Christianity "what Jesus does" depends upon "who Jesus is." A moment's thought should reveal that this interpretation robs the exemplary role of Jesus of both virtue and challenge. In this study we are suggesting that the order should be reversed so that "who Jesus (or anyone) is" depends upon "what Jesus (or anyone) does."

There are obvious hazards when anyone claims to be a christ without the preliminary proclamation. In doing so he assumes that he knows what others should find salvation to be. Even if his motives are evident and his judgment is reliable, even if he is a Jesus or a Krishna, he is still trespassing upon private territory. Each individual and group must be given the opportunity and responsibility to discern for itself what constitutes its noblest fulfillment, keeping in mind the legitimate claims of the larger community. But it goes without saying that in a pluralistic society no one can claim, in any sense, to be *the* christ. This is one of the most serious legitimate criticisms against traditional Christianity. By the same token, Islam must mature to the point where it can admit that there might be another interpretation of God besides Allah, and another prophet besides Muhammad.

The Christian Environment for Salvation. To speak of a christ as an agent in salvation is to think of it as a relationship or a "way." There are several christian ways. First, a christian relation can be one-way and from afar. Some might wish to deny that a one-way relation is a genuine relation on the assumption that all relations are reciprocal. Be that as it may, it is an empirical fact that one person may be a christ for another person or for a group without himself being aware of it. If salvation has been effected and an agent identified, the agent may be called a christ whether aware of it or not. X can be a christ to Y without knowing it, or without Y being a christ to X. Hence, we need to acknowledge a one-way christian relation.

Secondly, a christian relation may be mutual or two-way. This would be a real relation because it is reciprocated. In this case, X is a christ to Y and Y is a christ to X and each knows it. In this instance something very significant is added, the dimension of mutual depth of fulfillment and common salvation. Not only is a dimension added to both X and Y, but each finds himself included in a common objective orientation or environment of salvation.

Thirdly, a christian relation may also be three-way or multidimensional. In this case, three or more recognize themselves as involved in a salvation orientation where each is a christ for all and all are a christ for each and all. Just as the mutual or two-way has significant benefits absent from the one-way, so also the multidimensional has qualities all its own, aspects not present in the two-way. An obvious example of the mutual or two-way is genuine marriage; and a family would illustrate the three-way or multidimensional relation. Add children to a good marriage and you have the making of something which fulfills marriage in a unique way. The children bring something to the relation of each parent in the marriage. Other examples could be cited as well.

In the progression of the christian ways it is evident that when one establishes a multidimensional phase he has an environment that is especially loaded with salvation potential. Not only has he gone beyond previous phases in quantity, he has established an environment with a quality all its own. New potentialities appear; new relations come into play; new descriptions are essential; and a new level of being has been established, the reality that is the christian "church." To this theme we turn in the next chapter, assuming that it makes good sense now to speak of the secular christ as savior.

CHAPTER IV

The Secular Church
in Salvation

WITHOUT the preceding chapters as introductory the title of this chapter would be very puzzling. From a traditional point of view one cannot speak of a *secular* church in salvation because the word "secular" usually refers specifically to that which is nonchurch, nonecclesiastical and this-worldly. In contrast, the traditional Christian Church has been largely otherworldly, having as its primary purpose the preparation of the souls of the penitent for an eternal life beyond the grave rather than providing an abundant life in the here and now. The realms of the secular and the churchly were not only different in orientation, they were actually in competition with each other. Hence, any reference to a secular church in the traditional framework would appear to be a contradiction in terms. But the earlier chapters have shown that this is not a traditional orientation, and with them as introductory this chapter will try to show that there is no more contradiction in speaking of the secular church in salvation than in speaking of the secular christ as savior. The first phase of this task is establishing the secular church.

1. Establishing the Secular Church

It is evident from the concluding paragraphs of the preceding chapter that the notion of the secular church to be developed here is rooted in the notions of salvation and christ as already defined. In this introductory section we will try to indicate how the secular church is established through the christian relations, and then define the secular church in more detail.

The Christian Way to Church. The christian ways, as defined at the close of the preceding chapter, are clearly foundational in the process of salvation and in establishing the secular church. Even the one-way christ relation adds a new quality to life. Each of us has experienced this in one form or another. But when the christ relation becomes two-way or multifaceted a new horizon opens as one rises to a new level of life. It is a firsthand experience of an internal relation as defined earlier, and we are so much influenced by the relationship that we cannot be accurately understood apart from this christian event. It is literally constitutive of new being in the process of salvation; the new "we" and the new "me" must be understood as new in terms of this christian experience.

It is impossible to overemphasize the importance of the christ relation as foundational in the process of salvation. In unique and unforgettable ways it bridges the frequent chasms between persons and groups. We know, for example, that individual cells somehow overcome their cellular isolation in a larger functioning organism, and that to be understood as cells they must not be studied in total isolation from their organic environment. As organisms we have no conscious experience of this mysterious organic achievement. We do not even experience the functional interrelationships between the various systems within our bodies—digestive, respiratory, circulatory, and so on. But we can and do experience the christ event in which strangers become acquainted and the estranged are reunited. It is one of the overwhelming mysteries of life.

Contemplation of the christ event leads one to wonder: to what extent is an overarching or transcendental environment instrumental to the event? Has some attending presence beyond the two or more related persons come into play to make the christ event possible? Just as a certain disposition is essential for a cell to function within an organism, so also an appropriate attitude is essential on the part of each of those involved in a christ event. But can the full meaning or purpose of the christ event be understood in terms of the separate potentialities of the former "strangers" involved? We know from first-hand experience that the christ event establishes an environment that is both common and objective to those in the event. It is conceivable that an adequate understanding of the christ event requires the acknowledgment not only of the appropriate attitudes of the individual persons involved in the event but also an appropriate attending transcendental environment as well. As it continues this study will identify a series of transcendental environments with varying horizons. One of these is the secular church.

The Secular Church Defined. We are now in a position to define what we mean by the secular church. It is that multi-faceted christ-related group whose primary aim is to serve as environment for common salvation. As such it is a transcendental *social* level of reality that lays hold of appropriate new opportunities and new responsibilities. Just as a wheel opens a whole new area of potentiality that is not available to unassembled spokes, hubs, and rims, so also the level of reality that is the secular church opens entirely new vistas for creative development. All this is implicit in the notions of salvation and christ; apart from these notions the church has no meaning whatever. To call this church "secular" is only to emphasize that it is concerned with the short- and long-range possibilities of the here and now, assuming that the best functional orientation is the creative use of the present in relation to the past as remembered and the future as anticipated. When the secular church is understood in these terms, several pertinent features become apparent.

2. THE SECULAR CHURCH AS SAV*ing* AND SAV*ed*

Just as there are both instrumental and intrinsic aspects to the christ event, so also there are instrumental and intrinsic aspects to the church relationship or event. Each of these must be described in more detail by identifying the secular church as sav*ing* social agent and as sav*ed* community.

The Secular Church as Saving Social Agent. To suggest that there are various levels of reality, each with patterns of behavior that are peculiar to itself, is to imply that each level has potentialities that are equally unique to itself. Add to this the realization that the environment for salvation often involves a resistant or destructive element and one has the preliminaries to the notion of a social agent. Every aspect of reality seems to have its peculiar subjective aim, and every subjective aim encounters some concomitant resistant drag. The simple point being made here is this: every opportunity seems to be framed in a context that may facilitate or endanger its realization. Just as individuals may encounter detrimental aspects in their environment which they cannot overcome without the assistance of a christ, so also individuals and groups may encounter difficulties requiring the assistance of a "group christ," or church. In this sense the church provides an indispensable service for its own level of being. It is a social agent or instrument in salvation. By its very nature as a group it can achieve instrumental values that are not available through individuals as such. For example, the group therapy of Alcoholics Anonymous has often been successful after attempts by individual therapists have failed.

To identify the secular church as saving social agent is not to imply that all church activity should be viewed as therapy. There are some churches, such as Alcoholics Anonymous, which are organized for the sole purpose of correcting some specific sickness or sin, and their activities may be regarded as group therapy. But the activities of the secular church in this study usually involve more than rehabilitation from sickness or sin, as we will see in the discussion of worship. To suggest that the quest for secular salvation is the best clue to man is not to imply that man is "by nature" either sick or sinful. Rather, it is to suggest that for individuals, as for groups, man's "reach forever exceeds his grasp." He is a creature with a dream, a vision. In his imaginative and intimate relations with his fellows, as individuals and as groups, he provides an environment that is especially conducive to progressive creative fulfillment.

If we have these qualifications in mind, it is essential to point out that the saving aspect is the clue to understanding the secular church. The experience of salvation is such that man cannot avoid pursuing and expressing it. It is this basic impulse which leads to the church in the first place. The motivation is far more a desire to share something that is precious than to remove something that is horrible. When one discovers the christian benefits of these individual and group events, he naturally attempts to establish an environment that encourages their occurrence and development. The result is the secular church as saving social agent. But there is another natural dimension to the secular church.

The Secular Church as Saved Agency. While salvation is interpreted primarily as a process, it is not without its intrinsic benefits. Its quest is fulfilled when it is fulfilling, but memory testifies to the fact that it is fulfill*ed*, that there are those experiences which finish a phase of the creative process. Whether in the busy pace of Fifth Avenue or in the solitude of a remote mountain lake, we have group experiences that so overwhelm us as to leave us forever haunted by their power. They escape the current of change by providing renewed thrust and guidance. Years later we realize more fully the significance of that time and place and identify it as salvation achieved. We knew at the time that it was an hour that would pass when each must go his separate way, and yet we also knew it would bring to every opportunity for reverie its haunting quality. This is a church as saved agency.

Another example of the secular church as social salvation achieved is the event associated with the periodic reassembling of a group that knows itself to be a church. Each member, conscious of the benefits of previous similar events, eagerly anticipates the reunion in order to know the church experience as *now* and *new* once again. Though there continues to be change and growth, the point here is that an intrinsic reward has been won. Thus the church as salvation achieved is that uniting and reuniting group whose primary motivation and purpose is to stage the environment for the dramatic group salvation event.

To take the process of salvation seriously is to recognize that salvation achieved is the best foundation for continuing fulfilling development. History, nature, life—all are ongoing processes in which the context of the present shapes the turn of future events. Arranging the environment is obviously instrumental in the pattern of things to follow. Hence, the intrinsic benefits are also a clue to the meaning of the secular church.

No Salvation Outside a Secular Church. If there is any validity in what has been said, it would seem to follow that there is no lasting and evolving salvation outside a secular church. This does not mean that one cannot behold the ineffable through a fleeting christ relation or that one cannot recall the momentary with unusual benefit. But it does assume that much of the potential in a christ relationship will pass unrealized unless there is an appropriate enduring environment that serves both to preserve and to further utilize those potentialities. Moreover, apart from this attending environment some things precious would undoubtedly perish prematurely. The secular church is exactly that environment which seeks to develop the potential and preserve the precious in the process of salvation. Without it the quantity and quality of genuine satisfaction is clearly reduced.

Though it hardly needs to be added, a concluding point may avert some misunderstanding. To suggest that there is no salvation outside a church obviously does *not* mean what Cyprian, Augustine, or Aquinas meant in their discussions of this (*extra ecclesiam nulla salus*). To attempt to argue that there is no salvation outside my particular church or churches is silly parochialism. Man can no longer speak of *the* Church any more than he can speak of *the* Christ.

3. The Secular Church as the Body of Christs

One can speak of a church in a variety of ways, as sav*ing* social agent or as sav*ed* social agency. One can also speak of a church as a body of christ*s*. In this particular study this phrase has special meaning.

"Body of Christs" Defined. Since the traditional Christian

Church often refers to itself as "the Body of Christ," we need to clarify what is meant here. In traditional usage the Body of Christ may mean loyalty to Jesus as a person, loyalty to the teachings of Jesus, membership in the church of Jesus as Christ, participation in the sacraments, and so on. As implied in previous discussion, the usage here is far more general. To refer to the secular church as a body of christs means simply that it is a group of people involved in a multiple christ relation or christ event. Since the christ relation is functional, the substance or structure of the secular church is based entirely upon its function, namely, salvation. Hence, the church as a body of christs is only another way of saying that a group of people are functioning as a unity in the quest for secular salvation. The interpretation of salvation will vary from church to church. The traditional Christian interpretation may be one legitimate alternative, but under no circumstances can it claim to be the only legitimate christian interpretation. To repeat, man can no longer speak of *the* Church or *the* Christ any more than he can speak of *the* best move in chess. It is better to speak of a church as a body of christs.

The Secular Church as Sacred. In terms of its structure and its function the secular church is sacred. The word "sacred" has been used to refer to something "exclusively appropriated to some person or to some special purpose." We have seen that a secular christ refers to a special environment that includes both person and purpose and, hence, is sacred by definition. Since the secular church is composed of the body of christs, it is sacred in terms of its structure; and since its purpose is identical to that of the secular christ, though operative at the social level, it is sacred in terms of its function. Anyone who has been a member of a genuine secular church event knows the meaning and relevance of the secular church as sacred.

4. The Life of the Secular Church: Worship

The various nonsecular churches that exist today provide such a wide variety of services—educational, medical, counseling, social, and even business—that the service of worship seems almost incidental in comparison. Moreover, many contemporary Christians feel that these services are more important to society at large than is the service of worship and they will support these services financially while they limit their participation in the service of worship to Christmas and Easter. Many of those who attend regularly acknowledge that their reasons are not primarily liturgical but to support the fringe services.

In the secular christian church the service of worship is central. The aim of the secular church is providing fulfillment to life in the here and now in a form or fashion not provided by any other institution. Though the amount of time that is spent in worship is comparatively minimal, the benefits of that "sacred hour" are felt much longer. To illustrate the centrality of worship in the life of the secular christian church we need to define the term, to identify the roles of ritual and sacrament, and to show the significance of the liturgy and its fulfillment.

Worship Defined. From a functional point of view, worship refers to any church activity that is vital to its life. This approach allows for a great variety of forms, as it should. Since we have suggested repeatedly that the aim of the church may be satisfied in a number of ways, depending upon a specific church at a specific time, we have to acknowledge the possibility of a great variety of forms of worship. In this study, worship refers to any symbolic church behavior which *anticipates* or *expresses* secular salvation as we have defined it. Each of these aspects of worship needs a brief commentary.

Anticipation is vital to worship. It is the quest in its keenest form of hope or longing. To the sensitive spirit it is an appetite no less evident than hunger or thirst in the body, and it usually satisfies itself partly through prayer. Prayer, then, is the most deliberate and dedicated individual or social petitionary support for salvation as anticipated. It is petition under commitment. Though prayer is directed to that part of the environment which is acknowledged as most relevant to the satisfactory fulfilling of the supplication, and though the effort itself is deliberate, the attitude of those who pray is one of devoted abandonment. We suggested earlier that salvation, like happiness, usually cannot be quested for directly, but rather involves patient dedication and risk. So we might say that the expectation is indirect. Prayer is the culminating effort to order the environment for the benefits of Grace. It is anticipation without demand; it is longing with hope for response, but it is not a covenant arrangement where exacting litigation is conducted or where negotiation is relevant.

Worship is also the expression of salvation achieved, overt and direct acknowledgment of the benefits of the church. It is often the spontaneous recognition of prayer fulfilled. Where anticipation is satisfied beyond measure, there the testimony is charismatic and overwhelming. This is what is meant by praise, that is, spontaneous commitment with gratitude. Small wonder that worship so conceived as prayer and praise is central to life itself and often leads to stabilized patterns of behavior in ceremony and sacrament.

Ceremony and Sacrament. Ceremony refers to ordered symbolic church behavior that is directed toward a specific goal. Through it the bodies of the individuals become incorporated into a group body. In using his body one can go beyond the verbal and actually feel out in time and space, now and here, the meaning of the moment. Thus, involving the body in worship adds a third dimension otherwise lacking. Worship includes thought, but clear and compelling thought leads to action. The ceremony provides the body with the avenue for creative and active symbolic expression.

Sacrament refers to any ceremony that is deliberately designed for any occasion that is especially loaded with salvation potential. Clearly there are some occasions in life that merit some special ceremony to memorialize an event: the birth of one's child, the first day of school, initiation into the adult community (as in graduation from school, joining a church, or gaining the civil rights of voting, owning property, or driving a car), marriage, retirement, and death. There are also special times or seasons, such as springtime and harvest, the appearing of the new moon, and so on. Each of these, and others that could be added, are acknowledged as occasions with sacramental potential and hence deserving of special ceremonies that develop and express the deep latent feeling. The actual form of the ceremony in each case would depend upon the imaginations of the individuals, the attitudes of the churches, and other cultural factors of time and place. In any case, these are instances when we are especially receptive to expressive ceremonies—sacraments.

The Order of Worship and Its Fulfillment. If the quest for secular salvation is a reliable clue to the understanding of man both as an individual and as a part of a larger social structure, then worship, as we have defined it, would be man's most focal effort in staging the environment in order to elicit and express the maximum soteriological benefits. In other words, the worship service itself is arranged in such a way as to increase the probability of a significant experience. It deserves the most imaginative and persistent efforts because it is itself climactic.

To suggest that secular christian salvation is worship-centered and that the worship experience is climactic is to say that the greatest fulfillment in life comes in worship. Through the sacraments one can utilize the special events in life in such a way as to give meaning to all the intervening months and years. Hence, with a cultivated pattern of individual and group behavior one can gain satisfaction potential for the normal routines of daily living. The worship event is the pinnacle of living, the least ordinary of experiences, and its benefits extend to the horizons of both expectation and memory.

As meaningful patterns of worship persist they often find expression through the secular church in its temple.

5. The Secular Church and Its Temple

The events of life that are especially full of sacramental potential seem to lay hold of us and leave us restless until we develop a liturgy that gives adequate external expression to the inner feeling and fire. There seems to be a native need for developing symbolic ways of discharging the hidden internal energy. To do this a church requires an environment that is appropriate to the specific need. Typically, such an environment seems to include symbols, myths, scriptures, temples, and temple personnel. The function of each of these requires brief comment.

Symbols, Myths, and Scriptures. The basic need for symbols is rooted in the ineffability of the experience of salvation itself. Though the meaning of any experience tends to escape communication, the experience of salvation poses a real challenge. Words that are adequate for the task seem forever to fail us, and yet there is the irresistible desire to make its meaning known. Thus man needs to resort to the use of symbols.

By "symbol" we mean anything—word, object, event—that helps to explore and express the deeper levels of reality. In the language of the earlier chapters this means that a symbol is something which helps to discover and express the deeper and broader aspects of salvation. Paul Tillich has suggested that symbols "point beyond themselves," "participate in that to which they point," and not only "open up levels of reality which are otherwise closed to us" but also "unlock dimensions and elements of our soul which correspond to the dimensions and elements of reality."[32] Insofar as symbols serve as keys to unlock mysterious sanctuaries of meaning both within one's self and also in what appears to be a more external environment (and this in such a way as to establish an experience of greater satisfaction), to that extent one can say that symbols are, in the language of the earlier discussion, agents of salvation. The fact is that symbols do reveal *us* and *to us* areas of reality that otherwise would remain hidden. We have used the word "christ" to refer to the human agent in salvation and the word "church" to refer to the social agent in salvation. If "symbol" refers to any word, object, or event that is instrumental in salvation, then "christ" is a personal human symbol and "church" is a social symbol.

Though symbols have been defined and discussed in many different ways, our primary concern is with the symbol as that which helps to experience and express the otherwise ineffable aspects of the meaning of salvation. With this interpretation, symbols are vital to the life of the church and hence feature in its worship. In verbal form they give rise to myths.

Myths have always been vital in worship. From a historical point of view a myth is a story of unknown origin that usually utilizes a historical event to explain some significant aspect of the life of man. To indicate its specifically religious orientation its characters are usually gods or semidivine beings, dealing with a realm that is clearly supernatural and which clearly defies any definite location in space or time, in contrast with a legend whose characters are usually human and whose scene is set in some time and place. Myths, like symbols, have been defined and discussed in such a great variety of ways that we can do no more here than suggest the usage in this study.

In the present context, the interpretation of myth and its significance for worship is similar if not identical to the historical usage. Myths are stories that are imaginatively designed to explore and express the more profound depths of human experience. They root in individual or tribal events that defy simple historical description or classification. In other words, myths attempt to reveal a transhistorical quality or dimension which escapes simple identification of any one time or place. They attempt to touch something that is transcendental to and yet eternal in human life. In their telling and retelling they engage the creative imagination of man until historical event becomes mythological story. In terms of our earlier discussion, myths, like symbols, attempt to explore and express the ineffable aspects of the experience of salvation, and hence are vital to worship. In their content they utilize the equivalent of divine beings (christs) and refer to the transcendental (supernatural) realm.

Since the language and intention of myths are obviously symbolic, they should not be interpreted literally. Their form and content must always be understood in terms of their function. That is to say, a myth must always be understood as *a myth*. For example, Rudolf Bultmann has argued that the message of the New Testament has been misunderstood because too many

Christians have not acknowledged sufficiently its prescientific and mythological medium. It has been taken literally, and because of this, it is no longer meaningful to modern scientific man. Its form is obsolete. Hence, according to Bultmann, if the enduring truth of the gospel is to be made available to man again, it must undergo the process of "demythologization." The term is misleading in that it implies the removal of myth when actually Bultmann is advocating the renewal of myth or "remythologization." The use of myth in this study is clearly sympathetic to Bultmann's point of view if we have interpreted it correctly.[33] In any case, these instrumental and transcendental aspects of symbols and myths are vital to the life of the church in worship. This point should become even clearer in a discussion of scripture.

Scripture is the literature of salvation. It is the natural result of utilizing the literary form in attempting to express the impulse behind the origin of symbol or myth, the natural culmination of the attempt of the individual or church to express the significance of the christ or church event. Any literature that either triggers or transmits the experience of profound satisfaction may be referred to legitimately as scripture, whether at the individual or church levels. This is obviously a functional approach to scripture. Any literature that fills this function may be classified legitimately as scripture.

There are several important implications in the functional approach to scripture. First, there can be no fixed body of scripture, no "closed canon." Allowing for a variety of interpretations of salvation, christ, and church, and encouraging an evolutionary development in each of these aspects of experience, one must assume a fluid canon. Secondly, scripture should always be interpreted symbolically rather than literally. The closing of the canon in Christian church history was a strong stimulus toward the literal reading of the collection of sacred writings. The criteria used in the establishment of the canon presupposed a "substance" approach rather than a "functional" one. To assume, for example, that there was a definite period of divine inspiration in history, or that there was a sacred language, or that there were some specific individuals who alone were qualified to write scripture, and then to close the canon on these terms is to encourage a literal reading. The words become the Word, and the Word becomes an unchanging end in itself, leaving the reader with the impression that the original meaning is the only reliable one. To read scripture literally rather than symbolically is, as Tillich and others have seen, a form of idolatry, namely, bibliolatry.

Hence, thirdly, it follows that we must make a clear distinction between "Bible" on the one hand and "scripture" on the other. From the point of view of this study these terms are not synonymous. Just as traditional Christianity must learn to make a distinction between Jesus and christ, so also it must learn to make a corresponding distinction between Bible and scripture. Some of the Bible may continue to be scripture and some of it may not. We have argued that contemporary man must be free to decide for himself whether or not Jesus is a christ; so also contemporary man must be free to decide for himself which parts of the Bible, if any, are scripture. It may well be that many contemporary churches will continue to find the Bible, or parts of it, to be scripture, but in doing so they should be conscious of the distinction.

Finally, this functional approach to scripture may help to clarify the problem of authority. The first chapter included as one part of the current revolution in Christianity the notion of "the Bible without authority." It should be clear now why this was done. A significant proportion of Biblical literature is prescriptive and propositional in form, encouraging a literal reading. But many of its ethical prescriptions are now regarded as obsolete and many of its propositions are flatly contradictory. Small wonder that the authority of the Bible is being challenged. In contrast, the functional approach acknowledges that scripture is usually poetic or kerygmatic, and its authority must be understood accordingly. If it is prescriptive or propositional, it must endure the most careful scrutiny that is appropriate to that type of scientific literature. In any case, the authority of scripture is measured in terms of its contribution to the enrichment of the life of the individual or the church. To advocate the infallibility of either the Bible or scripture is to talk nonsense.

In summary, there are notable advantages in the functional approach. It keeps the scriptures alive and relevant; it may even help to restore some parts of Biblical literature to the status of scripture. For example, a literal reading of the New Testament accounts of either the birth or the resurrection of Jesus is ridiculous to modern man. To argue that the "star of Bethlehem" was a close conjunction of Jupiter and Saturn or a passage of Halley's comet, or that the "virgin birth" was some form of mysterious parthenogenesis or that the resurrection was some kind of unique and miraculous metamorphosis is to miss the point completely. A functional approach to myth and scripture interprets these accounts and others in an entirely different way. To illustrate this, assume the position of a Mary Magdalene. Suppose for the moment—and this is possible—that a man not only saved her from being stoned to death by a mob but in addition gave her life a meaning that overwhelmed her, forever escaping her comprehension. Suppose further, and this is also possible, that this man was later crucified and buried. Imagine Mary sitting in the garden near the tomb, waiting for the sun to rise, contemplating the life and death of this man. The sequence of events is recaptured in her memory with a clarity and power that had escaped her before, and she realizes momentarily the significance of what he had done *for her*. For her, the tomb could not consume the legacy of such a man. His influence continued to work its mysterious wonders. For her, he had been a christ. Surely the birth of such a savior would be of God, marked in the sky by a celestial light, and heralded by an angelic chorus. And would not one such as this rise to an eternal place of heavenly power where his wonders could be known throughout all the world?[34]

The point here is that the nature of the experience of salvation is such that it elicits from the individual or group the most imaginative efforts to express the overwhelming benefits of the sacred event. It is to be expected that the person or group involved will employ a symbol or language system that is already a part of its own life. Hence, if one believed in myths that told of virgin births, angels, miracles, stars that revealed divine purposes, resurrections from the dead, and the like, as marks of the unusual or significant, would he not naturally utilize these mythological rudiments in his attempt to express the ineffable? Scripture is written with imagination, and with imagination it should be read.

The Temple and Its Personnel. Just as the scriptures are man's noblest efforts to express the salvation event in literary form, so the temple is his attempt to provide a suitable place for the church to worship. Its location and design will play a significant symbolic function. Its architectural detail will reflect the church's attitude toward the fundamentals of worship. The temple will be designed in such a way as to provide the greatest opportunity to utilize a variety of forms in the celebration of the sacraments. The relation between religious faith and architecture has always been evident in temples, tabernacles, and cathedrals, and so it will continue. To the extent that one can assume a variety of interpretations of salvation, christ, church, and scripture, to that extent also one may assume a great variety of temple architectures.

Whatever the architecture, the temple will be a special space. To the extent that secular christian salvation is worship-centered and to the extent that the worship is associated with the temple, to that extent the temple will be a precious place. To the extent that the architecture and accommodations are instrumental to the worship, to that extent they will become a functional part of the church itself. In providing its symbolic environment its contribution is not restricted to the sanctuary. One emerges to find that the streets themselves become aisles and the sky an arching jeweled dome. Thus the temple becomes important in itself and the church must be on guard lest it become an end in itself, an idol.

Once a temple has been constructed, the church must make an important decision. Who will be responsible for the protection, maintenance, and general upkeep of the building? Will the group organize in such a way that specific persons will have specific responsibilities or will it remain a casual kind of relationship? We have seen that there are benefits in an "order of worship" as well as in spontaneity. If the church desires the benefits of order, organization, and stability, must it not of necessity relegate responsibilities in terms of abilities? Someone must make the temple ready for worship and someone must be in charge. Hence, the church must decide whether or not it will become an institution.

6. THE SECULAR CHURCH AS AN INSTITUTION

In any sophisticated church it becomes apparent very early that the advantages of orderly worship are the reward of disciplined efforts. Organization seems to be an inevitable part of sustained group activity. Just as salvation depends upon the creative ordering of the environment, so also the service of worship requires creative ordering, and this creative ordering seems to lead to an institution. This tendency can be detected after we define what we mean by an institution and then recognize the proclivity of the secular church to both expansion and permanence, to the need for a priesthood, and to involvement in the larger community.

An Institution Defined. To speak of the secular church as an institution means no more at this point than that it establishes organized patterns of behavior to meet characteristic individual and social needs. As suggested earlier, in this study we move from function to structure. When the purposes of the church become clear and the various ways of serving those purposes are established, then the order of the church gives it a form, and one may refer to it as an institution.

Natural Tendencies: Expansion, Permanence, and Specialization. The experience of secular salvation is such that man not only seeks it, he also seeks to share it with his fellows. This inclination is involved in the establishing of the secular church in the first place. Once established, the quest continues and hence gives rise to a natural expansion of membership. Salvation events seem to involve an inevitable evangelism, not in some crude proselytizing form employing psychological tricks or dubious motives, but rather in the sense of an intense desire to share what one regards as genuinely precious. There is no deliberate attempt to *persuade* or to *convert* because that kind of motivation presupposes an orthodox point of view that is assumed to be superior to others. The typical evangelist, whether political or religious, usually needs to do more listening and less shouting.

There are clear benefits in the expansion of the membership of the secular church when legitimate and sophisticated media are utilized. There is the natural thrill and excitement of great numbers of people sharing a profound type of experience. Moreover, in this day of mobility one expects a natural expansion from place to place, providing a comparison of a variety of types of worship experience. As members of a church move to another place they naturally seek out those with similar appreciations. Memory linkages unite one church with another, and the foundations for a denomination of churches are laid.

Though the benefits of such expansion are obvious, there are concomitant dangers in ever-expanding organizations. If it becomes large and impersonal, there is the threat that the *structure* will detract from the *function* or even lead to a new notion of the function in terms of perpetuating the structure. Needless to say, from the point of view of this study, that is tragic idolatry and should be avoided at *any* cost, even the sacrifice of the denomination. One needs to keep this in mind in a time when new emphases on superecumenism are being published abroad. The primary function of a secular church is worship, and any ecclesiastical structure that has some other goal in mind needs careful guarding.

Coupled with the natural tendency to expansion is a natural tendency to permanence. Just as there is a natural desire to share that which is most precious, so also there is a natural desire to preserve in memory and renew and develop in worship the experience of fulfillment. This tendency to preserve the precious can be seen in the development of myth and scripture, in the erection of temples of stone and stained glass. The scriptures tend to become "holy"; the sacred place becomes a shrine forever. We share our worship with our children and thus bridge the break between the generations and appear to defy time.

There are both benefits and dangers in this tendency to permanence. On the one hand, it provides the opportunity of establishing a tradition that adds temporal depth, of bequeathing a legacy as a means for identity, and, generally speaking, richer depths of meaning. On the other hand, in the face of change and challenge, the tradition tends to become orthodox, intolerant, and militant. As orthodoxy it claims to be an ultimate value that resists change because of an assumed eternal relevance and universal uniqueness. The pages of history flash a warning at that point, reflecting all too clearly the tendency of orthodoxy to justify any degree of brutality against any foe. If history must be made in terms of extremes, it would be better to build the temples with straw and heat them with bonfires, and write the scriptures in the sand at low tide. The importance of creative change in the life and longevity of a church can hardly be overemphasized. Hence, the emphasis in this study on the *secular*.

In addition to the natural tendencies toward expansion and permanence, there is a natural tendency toward specialization. The secular church would naturally utilize the special talents of its members in the order of worship, whether in music, dance, or word that is spoken or sung. Those with leadership abilities quickly demonstrate their advantages. This is a part of the expanding order of the church and merits more examination.

From Temple to Priesthood. If the secular church minimizes the values of the tendencies toward expansion, permanence, and specialization, it can avoid the complexities of a temple and of temple personnel. But combine the acknowledged advantages of ordered worship, expansion of membership, permanence of temple architecture and stability of membership, and the obvious benefits of specialization, and one has clearly established a need for special personnel to assume leadership responsibility. The immediate question for the secular church is, How specialized should the leadership become? Very few will doubt the benefits of specialization but all will acknowledge that the more specialized the leadership becomes the farther it moves from the membership as a whole. Since the secular christian church is built upon the foundation of mutual christ relations, it must take care not to encourage a chasm between clergy and laity lest the christ relation become unbalanced or even one-way.

The problematic aspects of the relation of clergy and laity come to the fore. Should there be a specialized clergy? Should there be a sacrament of ordination? If there is a specialized clergy, should they give full time to the work of the church worship? If they give full time, how are they to be housed, clothed, and fed? Should they be permitted to marry and have families who would also need some form of financial support? What about sickness and retirement benefits and homes for the aged clergy? Within the secular christian framework there would be a great variety of answers to these questions.

Simply posing these questions illustrates how an organized secular christian church cannot avoid involvement with state government if it builds a temple and establishes a priesthood. Temples require space and care; space and care involve taxes and salaries; taxes and salaries require officers and bank accounts. Hence, it is impossible to avoid involvement in the larger community.

The Secular Church and the Larger Community. It is evident from previous discussion that if the secular christian church becomes organized, it cannot escape influential relationships with a larger social context. Three questions are especially relevant. First, what is the relationship between a secular christian church and other churches, whether secular or traditional? To the extent that the quest for secular salvation is the clue to understanding modern man, and to the extent that the secular christian church is designed to fulfill that quest, to that extent it would appear that the natural tendency toward expansion would mean that eventually all men would be members of one great secular christian church. On the other hand, there are many different interpretations of salvation and hence many varieties of secular christian churches. As a multifaceted creature, man could be a member of many different secular christian churches. The relations between the various churches should be established and measured in terms of their contributions to the total process of salvation.

Secondly, what is the relationship between the secular christian churches and other institutions? We defined a secular church as a multidimensional christ-related group whose primary aim is to serve as social environment for salvation. We defined an institution as organized patterns of behavior to meet characteristic individual and social needs. A secular church may or may not be an institution, depending upon whether or not it is organized. The problem is, Does not the definition of "institution" imply that all institutions are churches? If the individual and social needs that the institution is designed to satisfy are in any sense focal in the meaningful life, as the word "needs" clearly implies, then meeting them is salvational and the corresponding institutions are churches by definition. At this point we have to acknowledge this ambiguity, but the next chapter will clarify this relationship.

Thirdly, what are the legitimate boundaries of the program of any church, secular or traditional? At the present time many religious organizations, churches and synagogues, are engaged in activities that are clearly educational, or are competing with business or are engaged in social welfare, or are even political. The most controversial area at the moment is the relation of race and civil rights. The question is not whether or not these activities are legitimate. Obviously, in their more refined forms they are essential. The question is whether or not they are a legitimate part of the program of a church. We have suggested that the function of the church is worship. Whether or not standing in a picket line or participating in a demonstration can be interpreted as worship remains to be seen. Before we can take sides we need to see whether or not there are other institutions that are better qualified to assume some of these responsibilities. To do that we need to investigate the secular community as christian.

CHAPTER V

The Secular Community
as Christian

FROM the comments in the preceding chapter it is evident that we need to move beyond the secular church in salvation. In the concluding section we touched upon the relationships between the church and other churches, and the church and other institutions. But in the discussion of the program of the church it was most obvious that we would need to expand the scope of the investigation to include the larger secular community. This chapter will try to show that the secular community has a complex soteriological function. To clarify and defend this thesis we will identify the need for the secular community and then illustrate the need in a brief examination of the various basic institutions.

1. ESTABLISHING THE SECULAR COMMUNITY

In ordinary language "the secular community" refers to the nonchurch or the nonecclesiastical aspects of our culture. Since the preceding chapter spoke of the secular church, the word "secular" is of little value in distinguishing the church from the larger secular community. Were it not for the desire to maintain the secular emphasis, the term could be omitted here and we could speak simply of the larger community. To illustrate the need for the secular community as well as its soteriological function we must point out that man is a multifaceted creature, that he established institutions to meet basic needs, and that the community is the social structure that makes the institutions possible.

Man as a Multifaceted Being. Since the second chapter we have been assuming that the quest for secular salvation is the best clue to man, both in his personal life and in his social relationships. He is a creature with a dream, a vision. He can forever imagine life and the world as being better than they are. His memory holds before him the luring call of the heights and his insight applies the vision to his future. His dreams are many and complex.

In his quest for the realization of his dreams man discovers early that he is a being with a number of needs. Some of them are essential to mere survival: food, shelter, reproduction, and rest. Once he advances beyond the survival level of existence and establishes a culture that removes the rudimentary threats to his life, he becomes more fussy about what he eats and how he lives, how he spends his leisure time, and so on. The tendency to fussiness leads the more fortunate and imaginative of men to develop new techniques for meeting old needs, and as leisure time increases, the latent cultural potentials find expression in a variety of ways. To satisfy his ever-increasing aesthetic longings man develops institutions.

Institutions and Human Needs. In the preceding chapter we defined an institution as an organized pattern of behavior to meet characteristic individual and social needs. We are assuming that all our basic institutions have been established to satisfy specific needs of man as those needs are identified. Institutions are a part of man's tendency toward specialization. The talented and initiated specialist can do a better job in meeting a need than can a layman. Since the institutions are designed to satisfy felt needs, and since needs and their satisfaction are central in the abundant life, institutions are vital to salvation. Most of this chapter will be devoted to a brief analysis of some of our key institutions—the family, the school, employment, leisure, and the state—as each and all are involved in the larger process of secular salvation.

The Secular Community as Agent. The secular community is the more or less unified and localized center of social activities. Like an institution, it involves orderly patterns of behavior to fill characteristic needs, but it is more than an institution in that it is a larger cultural matrix or environment in terms of which the various institutions function. Individual institutions are not autonomous or self-sufficient. They are specialized patterns of behavior with specific purposes. Each of them requires a larger dependable cultural environment in order to fill its specific role. Thus for their very existence the institutions depend upon the community. Just as the church is a social reality beyond the two-way christ relation, so also the community is a *whole* that is more than the sum of its parts (institutions).

Since each of the institutions fills a soteriological function and since the community is the more complex combination of the institutions, it follows that the secular community is clearly an agent in the process of salvation. The title of the chapter, "The Secular Community as *Christian*," and the titles of the sections within the chapter are designed to reflect the function as agent.

2. THE CHRISTIAN HOME AND FAMILY

Of all the institutions of modern man none is more immediately instrumental to the good life than is the family. By a family we mean the group consisting of parents and children, whether the children are genetic or adopted. The family group may include three or more generations. With this common-sense definition of a family it is not difficult to show that our patterns of living are very much oriented around the family group. As children we are totally dependent upon our parents, and our whole style of childhood life is formed and framed by parental modes. As parents we are concerned much of the time with the care of our children. A significant amount of both the anxiety and the satisfaction that a parent feels, especially the mother, relates directly to the maturation and happiness of the offspring. This is natural in a family-oriented culture. If these relations are right and rewarding, life is rich and joyful; if these closest relations are strained and irritating, life is correspondingly tedious. That our culture is family-oriented can be seen through a brief discussion of the role of the family and its relation to our future life.

The Role of the Family. To be an institution the family would have to meet certain characteristic needs. In the case of the family these needs are obvious and basic to survival—food, clothing, general residence, and normal tender loving care. To the family is delegated the responsibility of reproducing the species and the general rearing of children. It is within the family pattern, more specifically the husband-wife relationship, that adults are expected to find sexual expression and fulfillment. Indeed, sexual expression is uniquely important according to current law. We may eat, work, or play with anyone we please, but the intimacies of sex are regulated by law. Hence, one can say that this relationship is peculiar and special to the marriage covenant. Taken as a whole, the needs that are satisfied within the family structure are the most important of any felt by man. Thus, the next point follows logically.

The Family as Christian. After we have identified some of the obvious and yet basic needs that are filled by the family, it almost goes without saying that the family orientation provides an environment for fulfillment that is uniquely and inexpressibly precious. Both the frequency and the intimacy of family relations make the home a special kind of sanctuary. In such an environment the normal routines of daily life can assume a significance that is no less than sacramental, and the members of such a family are fortunate beyond any measure. In other words, the routine filling of these basic necessities is absolutely prerequisite to a satisfactory life.

In addition to the normal patterns of daily living there are several special events in the life of a family, the family sacraments, that deserve some elaboration. A sacrament we defined as any ceremony that was deliberately designed for occasions that were especially loaded with potential meaning. The sacrament is the symbolic ritual that is instrumental in bringing to fruition the salvation potentialities that would otherwise go unfulfilled. Obviously, no hard-and-fast lines can be drawn between the events that give rise to the sacraments and these special rituals which are associated with the special events. Just as there can be no clear demarcation between the reality behind a symbol and the symbol itself, so also there can be no rigid separation between the sacramental ritual and the sacramental event. One such event is *marriage*, the occasion that establishes a unique relationship between husband and wife. If a family is to be christian, the husband-wife bond must be a two-way christ relation. The wedding ceremony includes not only the covenant of bride and groom but also the cooperation of the larger community as well. All who know and love the bride and groom must honor their commitment in the interest of the mutual christ relationship. Secondly, there is the sacramental of *birth*. When the preparation is appropriate and the expectation adequate, the advent of a new life is cause for rejoicing. There is no end to the potential that is felt. The whole tribe longs for the fulfillment of all previous generations in this one new life. To fail to respond with imaginative ceremony and celebration on such an occasion would be an inexcusable sacrilege. *Death* is another sacramental. In a family-oriented society, death leaves its deepest sorrow in the family circle. Though in a different way, it is as overwhelming as birth. To behold one's parent or brother or betrothed in death, especially when premature, is to know an emotion that can never find adequate release except in symbolic ceremony. Vacations, reunions, and other times or seasons that are special to specific family groups merit an imaginative ritual that will nourish the memory and lure the heart to the hearth again. This is the family as christian.

The Family in Transition. The revolution referred to in the first chapter is not without its influence on the family. A number of factors are at work in our contemporary culture that will undoubtedly affect for good or ill the family of the future. Most important, probably, is the apparent relaxation of sexual restrictions along with improved methods of contraception. Greater general tolerance of divorce and remarriage are relevant to the family in a time of change. New willingness, even eagerness, to overcome childlessness by adoption or artificial insemination reflects an attitude of experimentation on the part of many responsible adults. Genetic breakthroughs promise to provide in the near future a form of human life far superior to that of the present or past. Boarding schools, summer camps, and other forms of socially acceptable family aids are also a part of the family in transition.

One of the questions with which the youth of today and tomorrow must reckon is: Is there an indispensable *family* function? Conceivably, each of the needs identified above can be satisfied outside the family orientation. One can dine and lodge very well in cafeterias and hotels. As for sex, man is obviously in a time of transition when he can have sex without either marriage or children and can have children without either marriage or sex. Moreover, cafeteria dining and hotel lodging are far less wasteful of precious food and space, and the advantages of sophisticated birth control and modern eugenics over present romantic practices are so obvious as to require no defense. The basic question is: Does the greatest fulfillment of human life depend upon the continuation of a family-oriented culture? Does man need the family as it is now defined to achieve the pinnacle of satisfaction? Is there a *family* will-to-meaning in the individual psyches of men? Although it is not part of the purpose of this study to attempt to answer these questions, they are vital in the development of the secular community of the future.

3. THE CHRISTIAN SCHOOL

Another institution that is vital to the well-being of our common life is the school. We will try to demonstrate its significance in the secular community by showing the need for the school, its role as secular and sacred, and a concluding comment on education and salvation.

The Need for the School. Both the nature of man and the nature of salvation point to the indispensability of education. Man is both natively curious and natively uninformed. He is the questioning animal and, as such, is frustrated until he receives some answers that satisfy his probing curiosity. The "How?" and "Why?" parts of man are aspects of this multifaceted creature that demand satisfaction in ever-expanding education.

The nature of salvation also requires education. Salvation involves both intrinsic and instrumental values. The intensity of the intrinsic value may seem to fix itself permanently in the shape of things, but actually the intrinsic value becomes instrumental in the quest for salvation. The quest is a process, a continuing development. Development requires direction and direction requires decision, the choosing between alternatives. Reliable decisions are essential and they require appropriate and accurate information—education. Thus the nature of man and the nature of salvation point to the indispensability of the school.

The need for the school, as identified above, has presupposed a definition. The school is the institution that is designed specifically to stimulate and satisfy the curiosity of man. Its purpose is to help man to become better acquainted with himself and his world, to provide the kind of educational background that enriches all experience. It is designed not only to answer his basic questions but also to encourage a deeper appreciation for every phase of life. The role of the school is vital to the process of salvation.

The School: Secular and Sacred. To speak of the school as secular is to continue an emphasis that persists throughout this study. The special meaning here is that it must be free from any sectarian control where the administration and/or curriculum is predisposed to some particular dogma or orthodoxy. Everyone associated with the operating of the school must be alert to the distinction between indoctrination on the one hand and objective presentation on the other. The danger in the parochial school is that enthusiasm may become proselytizing; the danger in the secular school is that objectivity may deteriorate into indifference. In the courses in science one must cultivate an attitude of detachment that prevents the coloring of the observation. In the courses involving norms and personal values one should practice the same detachment in trying to accumulate relevant data (evidence) and then commit oneself accordingly. Where the evidence is genuinely inconclusive one may appeal to personal aesthetic criteria which escape the scrutiny of logic. In any case, the normative secular school curriculum should include courses that are concerned with the basic issues of life—what they are, what the alternative approaches and solutions to them are, how to develop an ability to evaluate alternatives in a manner that is appropriate to the school environment, and so on. When all is said and done, one discovers that there is no substitute for the intrinsic value of *knowing* regardless of theological orientation or denominational affiliation.

When the school program functions as it should, the institution assumes a sacred dimension. The primary reason for the school as a school is to establish an environment for a special type of experience in the classroom. It is in the classroom that the teachers and students commit themselves to each other in cooperative creative research with an atmosphere of open and honest observation and dialogue. With proper motivation and stimulation, the student will find in the classroom the information and excitement that make his world come to life. At the more advanced and disciplined levels of study the revelations in the classroom and laboratory may have the same inspiring power as those in the temple or theater. When the inquiring mind comes upon a clue to the understanding of a larger part of the world, the excitement may be temporarily overwhelming. Such an experience adds to life a dimension of meaning that is uniquely precious. Nature and history are so full of fascination that there are no ends to their wonders! For those who have known this delight in the classroom, the school is sacred.

Education and Salvation. In conclusion it can be said that this is what it means to speak of the school as christian. It is an agent or instrument in opening avenues of appreciation. Education enriches all experience. Moreover, it is usually the disciplined and dedicated mind that beholds the revelation ineffable. Man is saved in no small measure through what he knows. The individual or institution that discourages or inhibits the creative process of enlightenment obviously does not know the dimension of its worth.

Current research in the areas of computerized teaching machines, talking typewriters, the "chemistry of learning," and the like makes one ponder with excitement the future of the school and the school of the future. The possibilities are certainly revolutionary. Whatever the form of the school of the future, its goals will be the same as the goals of the school of the past—to stimulate the imagination and inform the awareness of the student so that he can realize the best possible life.

4. Fulfillment in Employment

According to an ancient myth, man was created in the Garden of Eden. Eden seems to have been the ideal environment where man's every desire could be satisfied without any expenditure of effort. Then for some strange reason man offended the divine landlord and was evicted from the garden to discover to his deep regret that thereafter he could survive only through perspiration and pain. According to the myth, the need to labor and endure pain was the result of mischief and hence was a kind of curse upon man.

Whether or not the myth depicts any profound truth is a matter of personal opinion, but the fact is that today man cannot survive without working. Most of his days are spent in employment; he is vocationally oriented. To illustrate the relevance of employment to the general well-being of man we will discuss briefly the need for rewarding employment and the environment for a new Eden.

The Need for Rewarding Employment. Contemporary man is well aware of the fact that he must work. The minimal essentials for survival—food, shelter, and rest—demand a compulsory expenditure of effort. Besides, modern man is no longer willing to live on a survival basis. His expectations go far beyond his needs. Meeting these expectations requires an elaborate occupational institution.

Moreover, his *morale* seems to demand some form of productive employment. Though work may once have been interpreted as a curse, it is not so interpreted any longer. Since the time of the ancient myth our culture has felt the influence of Paul ("If any one will not work, let him not eat," II Thess. 3:10) and others who made a virtue of industry. In our culture, morale is so dependent upon productive employment that unemployment often leads to loss of respect or even delinquency, the very opposite of creative well-being.

The morale factor is the clue to the fact that man needs more than a job; he needs *rewarding* employment, and rewarding employment involves more than exercise, time consumption, and wages. Man's work relates him to a larger environment; it sets him against nature in the sense that he must resist the hostile forces of storm and disease that would destroy him; it aligns him with nature in that he can cultivate nature's bounty for the benefit of both himself and nature. He early discovers that nature will reveal her secrets to his inquiring mind and will bless his efforts if he will honor her. It is a cooperative enterprise, and man's work is not rewarding until he feels confident that he has made a contribution toward creative well-being. We have seen that salvation involves the creative ordering of the environment. Work attempts to do just that, and doing that is work. In this sense, work is man's attempt to put his creative design into the pattern of things, guided by his vision of beauty. This requires the expenditure of disciplined effort, and success in these attempts is very rewarding.

The Environment for Vocational Fulfillment. In order for work to be fulfilling in the sense just described we need to acknowledge that our complex human condition involves a hierarchy of responsibility and authority. For most workers today, the occupational satisfaction referred to must be found within these complex employment patterns. Several kinds of relationships must be kept in mind. First is the relation between the employ*er* and the employ*ee*. Each must recognize and acknowledge to the other the vital importance of morale. This means that each must attempt to provide for the other the environment for fulfilling employment. The fact is that each is a vital agent in the occupational satisfaction of the other. If either becomes unduly preoccupied with his own rights and benefits in isolation from the other, the chances of success are correspondingly reduced. The evidence for this is manifested daily in the newspapers.

A second relation, one that is closely associated with the first, is the relation between "work" and "wage." How is one ever to decide a rate of pay? The arbitrariness here can be seen through the illustration of the soldier who risks, and often gives, his life for his country. What is an appropriate pay? What is the appropriate wage for a lineman who braves a severe storm so that electric or telephone service may continue, or a roofer who repairs a leak before a precious ceiling is damaged or destroyed, or a surgeon or a priest who has spared one from appendicitis or suicide? One must conclude in each of these and other relations involving work and wage that no workman is worthy of his hire unless or until he is motivated by something beyond wages; and by the same token, no wage is adequate that does not include gratitude.

Admittedly, this is a romanticized view of vocational fulfillment. But why not? The term "vocation" refers to a career to which one has been "called," the assumption being that some divine power influenced the decision. At first the term was restricted to careers of full-time religious service, but as all work became more dignified it began to apply to any legitimate career. If a man's occupation proves to be sufficiently fulfilling and his theological viewpoint is appropriately flexible, he may well conclude that some celestial hand guided him into the specific career he pursued. In this discussion of work as fulfilling, we would like to see that environment established in which every worker would find such satisfaction in his efforts that he might be tempted to suppose that some significant contribution was being made to the creative well-being of man and that even the gods approved and were grateful. Any task that does not so contribute is not worth undertaking for any wage; one that does is worth any necessary sacrifice.

5. RE-CREATION THROUGH LEISURE

For the general well-being of man, leisure is as important as any other institution. To speak of leisure as an institution is not to identify it with the entertainment or resort business, though those endeavors are relevant as we will see. Rather, we are concerned here with the relationship between leisure and the good life of man, a relation that involves the vital need for leisure and the creative use of it.

The Vital Need for Leisure. Leisure may be defined as freedom from work. Work has a compulsory connotation; it is essential expenditure of effort because the situation demands it. Leisure refers to the time when one can feel free from forced occupation and do as he pleases.

Just as the human condition demands that man work, so also it requires that there be regular recesses from work. Unrelenting toil fatigues body and mind. Even when the vocation fulfills the life of man, he needs a break in the routine. It is not a mere truism that "all work and no play makes Jack a dull boy."

Moreover, there is an aspect of salvation that demands leisure time. We have seen that man must order his environment creatively if he is to know the benefits of cultivated living. This is work. But we have also seen that salvation is a gift of Grace. Some of the most precious types of human experience come only during a state of repose. Repose is more than resting from physical exhaustion; it is placing a rested body and an alert mind at the disposal of casual sensation, observation, and reflection. These are the moments that invite the ecstasy of selected memories, the heart "dancing with the daffodils." There is hope today that more and more people may know this kind of repose.

The Problem of Leisure. One of the most significant aspects of the current revolution is the marked increase of leisure. There was a time when leisure was the luxury of the wealthy few. Now machines and computers are doing more and more of the strenuous and tedious work. This means not only that man's working day has grown shorter and shorter but also that the tasks involve less effort and drudgery. Hence, the working man no longer needs to use all his free time for resting. This increase of leisure, while necessary to re-creation, may be a curse as well as a blessing.

It appears that, as a culture, we are not yet ready for this increased leisure. As sons of the Western Christian tradition we are still work-oriented and prone to feelings of guilt when we are not productively occupied. In the language of Harvey Cox, we need to "emancipate work from religion." Work is not yet "secularized." "Technopolis demands a new definition of work."[35] While some are poverty-stricken, others are leisure-stricken. We are still prone to "acute leisure-itis" and the "weekend neurosis." There is evidence that most suicides occur during weekends, holidays, and vacations.[36] It is generally agreed that boredom, or the inability to deal with leisure, is a factor in much juvenile delinquency and crime. It is true that "all work and no play makes Jack a dull boy," but it appears that there are even greater dangers in Jack's having a lot of free time with no designs for it.

Leisure as Re-creation. There is every reason to believe that in the decades ahead more and more people will have more and more time on their hands. With a mushrooming population, more automation and computerized machines, a shorter work week and an earlier retirement, and a longer life expectancy, there will be a marked increase in leisure time. If free time is to be a blessing rather than a curse, man simply has to learn how to handle it creatively.

The creative use of leisure requires careful preparation. It may well be that the transition from the work-oriented culture to the work/play-oriented culture will require more imagination and disciplined effort (work) than the old work/sleep routine. But man has no choice. Whether he likes it or not, there is going to be more free time. The only solution is the proper preparation in the secular community as a whole. This means providing ample and appropriate physical facilities, such as parks, playgrounds, resorts, and the like where people in great numbers can engage in strenuous unproductive fun. Fun is an end in itself and strenuous exercise helps to keep the body in good condition—a prerequisite to happy leisure. It means also the provision of facilities and programs that keep the mind alert and intrigued. The public library and school system can make an invaluable contribution by making good reading materials easily available and by providing classes for all ages in a wide variety of subjects, from developing hobbies to technical courses in government and religion. Entertainment is essential but not enough in itself. Television can be an inexhaustible resource. Just as the physical facilities are designed primarily to keep the body physically fit, so the programs of the library and school attempt to keep the mind informed and alert. Both of these aspects are essential. The primary function of the combined efforts is the development of inner resources so that the adult years, especially the retirement period, have some culminating and fulfilling role.

From these introductory remarks it should be clear why we link leisure with re-creation. Re-creation refers to the process of being created anew or afresh. The hyphen is important. Recreation, without the hyphen, suggests diversion or amusement or entertainment. Re-creation is more than entertaining what one is; it is the overhauling of life in such a way as to add new dimensions of appreciation. This does not mean that it is studied or compulsory; that would be work. As leisure it is a casual exposure to beauty and an adventure with spontaneity. It is the invitation to renewal through the abandonment to Grace. It is the peak of a*mus*ement that is also a*maze*ment.

6. The State as Coordinating Institution

Before the various institutions can function in such a way as to provide a secular community, some form of coordinating agency is essential. Each of the institutions discussed is designed to meet certain characteristic needs, and hence each is to that extent specialized. Moreover, these various institutions are interdependent. With few exceptions the individual human being participates in all of them. Sometimes the interests of the various institutions conflict, and at that point there must be an authoritative coordinating agency. We will identify the state as that supreme institution.

The Purpose of the State. The "state" is understood here in its usual sense. It refers to any political structure or government that assumes ultimate responsibility and exercises supreme authority within a defined geographical territory. In this sense it is a sovereign entity whose basic forms and functions are internally established. The power structure may be centralized in one or a few individuals or reside within the general citizenry, but to be a state there must be a stable pattern of government to meet specific needs.

The need for government is evident in even the smallest groups. Where there is any freedom of behavior there is likely to be disagreement, and where there is disagreement there must be some mutually acceptable means for solving disputes. At the national level the need for government is so obvious as to require no defense. In addition to government there is clear need for police protection from any enemies either domestic or foreign. The state provides for general order and control and regulates behavior where local authorities are ineffective. The state is the largest sovereign secular community.

The purpose of the state goes beyond the minimal needs of protection and control. As man moves from barbarism to cultivated civilization the needs for protection and control become less and less and the nobler purposes of the state begin to appear. Hence, the purpose of the state in a civilized community is to provide conditions for creative relationships between individuals and institutions within its political domain. In a sense this is a form of control, but the point to be emphasized is not control in the sense of manipulating human conduct. Rather, it is to utilize opportunities and exercise authorities which establish a national environment that most encourages conditions which make for creative well-being and the general welfare. The state is the superinstitution that coordinates the efforts of individuals, institutions, and secular communities in the realization of man's noblest aims.

The Individual and the State. It goes without saying that the state must have supreme control according to the law. This does not mean that the individual has no rights, but it does mean that the individual has no unqualified inalienable rights. No citizen can claim as his inalienable right any action that robs other citizens of the same rights. In any irreconcilable dispute between a citizen and a state, the state obviously must have pre-eminence. If it becomes a matter of extremes, the tyranny of order is to be preferred to the utter frustration of chaos.

It also goes without saying that the individual citizen must have the right to challenge the state under due process of law. But he must honor the law as *law* or, once again, the state will have no authority and even the minimal needs of the citizenry will be jeopardized. Our own times have seen the flagrant violations of the rights of individual citizens in Nazi Germany under Hitler and equally flagrant violations of the rights of government and of citizens in race riots and other forms of civil disobedience. If both the general citizenry and their government will keep in mind the purpose of the state as here defined, both of these extremes of flagrant violation will be avoided.

The State and Other Institutions. Our purpose here is not to discuss the state as one institution among others or even to identify it as first among equals. In referring to the state as the coordinating institution we are suggesting that it has a unique function in the secular community as christian. Each of the other institutions has been discussed in such a way as to show its special contribution to the abundant life. The point here is that the state also has a special role. Insofar as it involves patterns of behavior that meet characteristic needs, it is an institution; but insofar as it serves to establish an environment in terms of which the other institutions function, it is a superinstitution. Our present concern is limited to this function of the state in relation to the other institutions. (Here we continue to tread on very controversial territory without adequate space to defend some of the points suggested. Hence, it should be understood that the comments that follow are more for initiating discussion and reform than for persuading to a specific point of view.)

First, the state and the church. The church is one institution among others and, as such, deserves no special treatment. As an institution that owns property it should be taxed as is any other real estate. If it engages in business enterprises, it should compete on a fair basis with similar businesses and be held to the same standards and demands as other businesses. If it establishes special schools, the standards of these schools should be established and regulated by the state. In short, as soon as the church becomes an institution and functions as such in the secular community it should have no special privileges but rather submit itself to the state authorities.

Secondly, the state and the family. The family, like the church, is part of a larger community and should acknowledge as much. When it does, a variety of problems can arise as to jurisdictional authority. For example, has the state a right to decide who may marry and have children? Some citizens are clearly unable to assume the normal responsibilities of parenthood. If the state must assume the care of the offspring, has it not the right to decide whether or not there will be offspring? If a child suffers from a disease that will be fatal if not treated, has the state the right to take the child from parents whose religious convictions are opposed to any form of medication? Should a child be forced to be born or to die because of the convictions of its parents? Or if the family or friends of someone who is incurably ill cannot afford the medical expenses, has the state a right to practice euthanasia? "The man who pays the fiddler calls the tune." Why not?

Thirdly, what about the relationship between the state and the school? The school is absolutely essential to a civilized society and a stable state. In most cases it is state-supported. Has not the state both the authority and the responsibility of setting standards and providing facilities? If schools are state-supported, then should they not be state-controlled? ("No taxation without representation.") Moreover, does not the state have the right and responsibility to integrate its schools along academic lines? Can it send a child to a school regardless of the race, religion, or political persuasion of the parents?

Fourthly, what is the relationship between the state and employment? If the state is expected to provide specific services such as fire and police protection, unemployment benefits, social security, medicare, and the like, then it must have some dependable source of revenue for these purposes, such as taxation. But the more controversial questions revolve around the government's involvement in or control of business, fixing prices, establishing a minimum hourly wage or annual income, working conditions, and the like. In the disputes between labor and management the government, or some agency acting in that capacity, must have the opportunity and the authority to arbitrate.

Finally, what is the role of the state when it comes to leisure? Can the state require that all citizens have at least a minimum of leisure as well as a minimum annual income? Is it the responsibility of the state to make certain that there are adequate and appropriate facilities for leisure benefits? If so, has the state the authority to preempt private property to establish tax-supported public parks and beaches? And what about the resulting competition between state-operated and privately run resorts or recreational areas?

Obviously there will be enthusiastic differences of opinion on all these questions. They deal with the basic issues of life. All we can hope to illustrate here is the necessity of having some agency that serves as supreme judge in the areas of controversy in order to provide the most propitious total environment for the good life of all the citizenry.

The State and Other States. The same teleological principle that justifies the uniting of institutions into communities and communities into states seems to apply to the organization of states as well. Modern man has reached the point when domestic policies in one state affect the foreign policies of another. The test of nuclear devices by any state affects the atmosphere of the entire earth. The revolutionary advances in communication and transportation have thrust the entire planet into a new era of international negotiation. There was a time when the power of any government depended entirely upon the willingness of its citizens to obey and execute its policies. But today, as Henry Nelson Wieman has stated eloquently,

the power of any government is measured not only by the loyalty of its own people but also and increasingly by the number of different people beyond its own jurisdiction who are willing to cooperate with it. The wider the response of the people of the world to the announced and practiced policies of any government, the greater the power of that government.[37]

This means that modern man stands on the threshold of a new era in international relations. Nations that have thought of themselves as sovereign states are discovering a loss of that sovereignty to an international authority embodied in an organization such as the United Nations. The nations of the earth must ultimately unite into a functioning democracy. We can imagine the evolution of such a government only with difficulty, but it is the thesis of this study that, whatever the form, it will be conceived and developed eventually along man's vision of the good life for the planet as a whole. Just as the quest for secular salvation is the guiding map and the evaluating norm for church, family, school, work, and play, so also is it for the state and, eventually, the international union of states. In time, the same vision may need to be utilized in relating this planet with other planets.

7. THE SECULAR CHRISTIAN COMMUNITY

The secular christian community refers to any unified and localized center of social activities that is specifically and consciously instrumental in fulfilling an important aim or purpose. To be a "community" there must be a more or less integrated matrix of social engagement which each individual member would recognize as such were his attention drawn to it. To be "christian" it must be instrumental in the achieving of some intrinsic benefit which, again, each one would be able to acknowledge as such were his attention drawn to it. And to be "secular" it must involve benefits the intrinsic quality of which is at least partly evident in the here and now. Clearly, there are many such communities.

Summary and Conclusion. Several points need to be made by way of summary and conclusion. First, the boundaries of any secular christian community are relative to its aim or purpose. It may refer to a small village, a metropolitan unity, or an international organization. The boundary, geographical or functional, depends upon the context in which the need is conceived. Secondly, if the boundaries of any specific community are relative to the community function, it follows that the functions must be specialized. Since every function entails an appropriate cooperating environment, the distinction between institutions and communities can be made in terms of both specific functions and related environments. Since they are stabilized patterns of social behavior that meet certain needs, communities are complex institutions. The primary difference is that they function on a broader and more complex though less intimate social level. This distinction may be clearer if we relate a church and an institution, a relation that needs to be made according to the concluding paragraphs of the preceding chapter.

The primary distinction between an institution and a church is the intimacy of its internal relations. If one argues that all institutions meet needs that are vital to the abundant life, then one is saying that all institutions are churches. But this is the case only if the component parts of the institution are so mutually interrelated and interdependent that each derives its worth from the function of all the others, and if the functioning of the institution has all the meaning and power of worship as defined earlier. Usually the relations are not that intimate and committed. Some institutions may become churches just as some churches may become sufficiently organized to be institutions, but the terms are not synonymous except in regard to their general soteriological purpose. And in those terms all churches, institutions, and communities have a common goal—contribution to life fulfillment. Hence the title of this chapter: the secular community as *christian*.

Transition to the Next Chapter. In the preceding chapters and in this one we have attempted to identify a natural progression from the simpler to the more complex levels of reality. For example, we have moved from the electron to the atom, to the molecule, to the cell, to the human organism, the church, the community, the state, and finally to the international organization of nations. We have argued that each seems to have an identifiable reality of its own, yet at the same time each seems to be involved in the reality of the others. Thus we have to acknowledge that we are unable to circumscribe with any certainty the specific environment that is relevant to any or to all. The mystery of internal and external relations remains. It may well be that each requires not only all the others in order to be what it is, but each may also depend upon a larger and deeper environment not yet identified. We have seen that the christ relations at every level assume and imply an aspect in the environment that is felt but not faced, relevant but hidden. In and beyond the agent, there is Grace. To explore this we must move on to God.

CHAPTER VI

God and the
Secular Christian Life

NO discussion of salvation is complete without some reference to God. Early in the exploration we discovered that
salvation involved both agent and Grace. In the intervening
chapters we have attempted to characterize some of the more
significant aspects of the function of the agent as "christ" and
"church" and "community." Now we will see that God is the
special agent who accounts for the gift of Grace. To define and
defend the place of God in the secular christian life we will
identify several specific generations in the historical development of the notions of God, then note the important transition
from the notion of salvation to a conception of God that seems
to derive from it, and then, illustrate the significant phases of
God's incarnation within the process of salvation in christ,
church, community, nature, and history.

1. THE GENEALOGY OF GOD

A genealogy is a history of the descent of someone from his
ancestors. It is a pedigree of lineage that lists by name in
chronological order all the known generations between the
current one and the earliest one—father, grandfather, great-
grandfather, and so on. To suggest that such a notion can be
applied to God is likely to offend the orthodox, but careful
study of the history of religion indicates that this is the case.
There are some typical generations in the genealogy of God.

Some Typical Generations of Gods. The history of religion

shows that man is incurably religious. His religious experience is invariably associated with some sense of values, and with devotion or dedication to the source of those values. In a preliminary way we will suggest that it is sufficient for present purposes to identify God with the "objective source and conserver of values." In other words, for the purpose of identifying various typical generations, we will use as our basic and general conception of God "the objective source and conserver of values."[38]

The objective source of value may be understood in a variety of ways. First, God may be interpreted as "personified particular value" in which case there are many gods, "each god regarded as a vaguely personal (or impersonal mana) spirit which is the source of some energy which brings value to man. There are gods of rivers, springs, trees, rains; of fertility, of motherhood, . . . love, . . . war, . . . hunting, . . . and of truth." This is polytheism, the belief in many legitimate gods.

Secondly, God may be understood as "personified national spirit." This conception of god is rooted in the notion that "as civilization advances, men become more intelligently conscious of the coalescence of their various values, and polytheism tends toward some sort of unity." Man's values are closely associated with his cultural and political life, and "as the national life becomes more closely organized under one supreme monarch, so the pantheon (the hierarchy of all the gods) becomes more closely organized under one supreme god." This general point of view is referred to as henotheism, acknowledging the legitimate existence of many gods but restricting worship to only one.

When it was discovered that some of the religious myths (especially the creation myths) defied national boundaries and illustrated a conflict of both role and domain among the gods, man had to move beyond henotheism to monotheism. Moreover, when man discovered that there were some values that were common to every nation or tribe, he was led to suspect that they had a common source which did not apply to national or geographical boundaries. "The inevitable inference from all this was that there is only one God. Such was the outcome of the highest religious thought of Egypt, of Israel, of India, of Greece, and of Rome."[39]

Historically, this is a kind of genealogy for God. The transition from polytheism to henotheism and from henotheism to monotheism involves changes sufficiently distinct to permit one to refer to the historical phases as generations. Each phase has its own name; each is clearly rooted in the earlier phases, and yet each is sufficiently distinct to function in its own way. Hence, it is called a "genealogy."

This same genealogy is found in Biblical literature.

The Genealogy of God in Biblical Literature. When we utilize the results of Biblical scholarship and study Biblical literature in chronological and cultural perspective, we discover that the genealogical transitions from polytheism to henotheism and from henotheism to monotheism are clearly evident in the evolution of the religion of ancient Israel. To illustrate, the religion of the patriarchs was polytheistic according to both the Biblical texts and the archaeological evidence. The name for God in the so-called E source is a plural form, "Elohim." There were many "Els." After Jacob had his famous dream he believed that the rock supporting his head was inhabited by a spirit, so he named the place "Beth-el," or "house of an El," to honor that specific El (Gen. 28:18–19). His relations with his Uncle Laban clearly reflect an animistic polytheistic religion. (Gen., chs. 30 and 31.)

The religion of Moses, some five centuries later, was henotheistic. He made a covenant with Yahweh, the mountain man, a covenant that reflects a henotheistic tribal religion. The covenant and the Decalogue demanded that the followers of Moses have no god before Yahweh. Yahweh had chosen this tribe and he was to be the foremost god of this tribe. Other tribes had their gods: Chemosh for the Moabites, Dagon for the Philistines, Milcom for the Ammonites, Rimmon for the Syrians, and so on (I Kings 11:5, 33; II Kings 5:18; and 23:13). Just as the followers of Moses were chosen in the eyes of Yahweh, so also the other tribes were special in the eyes of their respective gods. Both Yahweh and Moses acknowledge the legitimate existence of other gods, but the worship in the tribe of Moses is to be restricted to Yahweh first. This is the generation of henotheism.

The contest that Elijah staged on Mt. Carmel (I Kings, ch. 18) dramatizes a period of transition in both a way of life and in religious beliefs. Prior to the conquest of Canaan under the leadership of Joshua the peoples of this land had an agricultural orientation with gods appropriate to their needs. Their deities, called Baals, had both territorial jurisdictions and fertility functions. After the conquest of Canaan the followers of Moses changed from a nomadic to an agricultural way of life. In adopting and adapting a new way of life there was the strong temptation to utilize the gods of the land. So these sons of Jacob had to decide which god they would utilize for which purpose. Naturally there was a conflict of franchise among the gods—"I the Lord your God am a jealous God" (Deut. 5:9)— so Elijah staged the contest to decide once and for all who the victorious god would be. (Using fire to decide was hardly fair, since Yahweh was a god of fire and the Baals were not.) The contest illustrates that the times were transitional and that the next generation in the genealogy was soon to appear.

Five centuries after the time of Moses there is a well-developed ethical monotheism in the religion of Israel. Each of the great prophets contributed significantly to this evolutionary advance. Amos emphasized a righteous judgment of *all* the nations, suggesting that God is both just and universal. Hosea tempered this judgment with love. Isaiah added the dimension of holiness. Jeremiah saw that these developments called for a new covenant because Israel now had a new and different God. (Jer., ch. 31.) In the prophecy of Deutero-Isaiah (about 580 B.C.), the religion of Israel reaches the new generation of ethical monotheism, and God is now One Universal Ethical Sovereign who expects appropriate ethical behavior on the part of all mankind.

By the time of Jesus, some five centuries after Deutero-Isaiah, God is clearly associated with the *heavens*. How God rose to this lofty height is now clear. From the mountain of Sinai to the territory of Canaan, through the fertility functions of sun and rain which honor neither national nor moral boundaries, God became the inhabitant of the heavens, from whence comes sunshine and rain. Both the religion *of* Jesus and the later religion *about* Jesus have much to do with this one universal God who is eternal in the heavens.

One may conclude, without doubt, that there was significant genealogical transition in the two thousand years that gave rise to the literature of the Old Testament. The God of Moses is not the same god as the gods of Jacob, and the God of Jeremiah is not the same god as the God of Moses. Each of the generations seems to have taken some five or more centuries, but those of us who have the historical advantage of looking back over the intervening millennia can clearly distinguish the separate generations here referred to as the genealogy of God.

By the same token one ought not to assume that the genealogical process will stop at the point of Jesus. In the two millennia since Jesus there have been many scientific and cultural advances that have required the continuation of the genealogical process. It is only natural to assume, then, that there will be periods from time to time that are markedly transitional. The current times seem to be just such a period.

The Current Transition: "Death of God" Theology. Just as man is incurably religious, forever fashioning for himself some reliable notion of God, so also he is incurably speculative and philosophical, forever fashioning for himself a reliable and relevant world view. One characteristic of the secular age is man's realization that his notion of God is subordinate to or a part of his larger world view. As his general life orientation changes, so also his notion of God must adapt accordingly. This is the evolutionary cultural process that we have seen at work in the genealogy of God.

It hardly needs to be pointed out that in a genealogy there is a genuine passing of the generations. New ones appear and old ones die. Similarly, when a prophet attempts to establish a new life orientation, the older notions that shaped the present lifestyle must pass in order to make way for the new. In order for the God of Moses to shape the life and destiny of that tribe the gods of Jacob had to pass, and in order for the new covenant of Jeremiah to mold the life of his time, the old God (Yahweh) and the old covenant of Moses had to die of neglect or be re-interpreted out of existence. And when Jesus emphasizes re-peatedly, "You have heard that it was said to the men of old, . . . but I say unto you . . ." (Matt., ch. 5), he is literally im-posing the death sentence on the older covenant and the older notions of God. While the text may claim that he came "not to abolish the law but to fulfill it," later history seems to pro-nounce the abolishment in the fulfillment. With new times, new covenants and new gods appear. The notion of the "death of god" is not new.

The primary problem with the current brand of "death of God" theology is that it does not make clear what it means by *the death of God*. Thomas J. J. Altizer and William Hamilton have listed ten possible meanings of the phrase in the preface to their *Radical Theology and the Death of God*.[40] While they choose the second possibility, namely, "that there once was a God to whom adoration, praise and trust were appropriate, possible, and even necessary, but that now there is no such God," they do not define and discuss it coherently and com-pletely enough to separate it from some of the other possibil-ities which in fact challenge it. If the radical theologian really believes that "God has died in our time," he ought to make plain what he means by "God" and "died." He should indicate, as he says, "why this change took place, when it took place, and who was responsible for it." This he clearly fails to do.[41] This is important because it determines whether or not one joins the ranks of the radical theologians. If, on the one hand, it means that the traditional Christian conception of God is now obsolete and must be replaced in temple and street, many of us would agree with enthusiasm. On the other hand, if it means that God as transcendental creative power has now ceased to function, or that every possible notion of God is now intrinsically meaningless and forever incapable of relevant interpretation, then we dismiss it as ridiculous and silly. To make a contribution to our transitional times the radical theologian must make his position clear.

Conclusion: The Need for a New "Generation." Our revolutionary times are clearly calling for a new "generation" in the genealogy of God. For a number of years philosophers such as Alfred North Whitehead, Henry Nelson Wieman, and Charles Hartshorne, and theologians such as Paul Tillich and Rudolf Bultmann—to mention only a few—have been trying to show the inadequacy of the traditional Christian conceptions. A modern world view has replaced the medieval world view, and the consequences are enormous for both religion and ethics. The widespread response to Bishop Robinson's *Honest to God* and the initial enthusiastic reaction to the "death of God" theology indicate that the need for a new generation in the genealogy has reached the popular level also. This chapter hopes to make a modest contribution to this need.

But before turning to a discussion of the concept of God we need to make several brief acknowledgments. First, the call for a new generation in the genealogy of God does not come from every sector of the population. There are still many people for whom there is no felt need to go beyond traditional Christianity, and one must avoid giving the impression that everyone *should* embrace a new notion of God. Every layman need not be speculative in theology, but if he becomes thoughtful and critical, he will discover that he needs to push for a new generation. Secondly, when most people talk about God they assume that there is an *objective* reality that exactly fits their conception. Yet when we compare our various conceptions of God we find that they are so diverse as to be contradictory. Obviously, then, there cannot be an objective God for every subjective notion. Thus it appears that when we speak about God we are saying as much about ourselves as we are about God. Small wonder that many an alert student will ask, after studying the history of religion, "Did God create man, or did man create God?" Each seems to make a notable contribution in the creative process. Thirdly, current theological literature continues to offer new and challenging options in the next generation in the genealogy of God. Since this study does not find any of them to be totally adequate, it offers another, realizing that many will find this one unsatisfactory. In any case, the dialogue is beneficial.

2. From Salvation to God

From the discussion above it appears that some conceptions of God are obsolete for some people in our times while others are not. It is the ambitious task of this section to identify a notion of God that is relevant to the secular christian life. To do this we will identify a soteriological approach to the notion of God, the agent and Grace as clues to God, and then develop briefly a notion of God as abstract noun and as proper name.

The Soteriological Approach to God. The history of religious thought includes a number of arguments for the existence of God—the ontological, cosmological, teleological, and so on. These arguments have been developed in a number of ways as every student of Western religious history is aware. Whatever their specific form, they usually utilize either the rationalistic or the empirical approach, or a combination of these. Since the soteriological approach assumed here is a combination of these, each must be identified briefly.

The rationalistic approach gives priority to conception over perception. This means that in his approach to God the rationalist would attempt to establish a clear, coherent, and inclusive notion of God. He might well ask himself, "What are the minimum characteristics of an adequate conception of God?" Or, "What must God be in order to be God?" There would then follow a logically consistent rationally developed conception. Regardless of the coherence and detail, one problem would persist throughout: Does such (a) Being exist? Is there any *actual* reality in the universe that accurately corresponds to the conception in the rationalist's mind? And what would constitute convincing proof? To be consistent this approach must limit itself to the logical priority and connectedness of concepts in the mind. If these can be sufficiently coherent and detailed, the conceiver may be persuaded beyond the shadow of doubt, but a number of notable philosophers, especially Immanuel Kant, have shown the limitations of this approach.

In contrast, the empiricist begins with experience and works toward the notion. Rather than begin with some basic conception from which one deduces the existence of God or, to put it crudely if not misleadingly, begin with the notion and then look for the evidence, the empiricist begins with the evidence and moves inductively to the conception. Technically, one could begin with any experience, or all experience in sum, and argue his way to God, as Whitehead does, for example. But usually one selects some specific experience that is especially revealing and then tries to account for it by appealing to other experience or all experience. This usually leads him beyond the realm of elementary experience to more sophisticated realms where he finds an adequate principle of explanation. Thus the experience of *cause* has led to the development of a cosmological argument, *purpose* to the teleological argument, *beauty* to the aesthetic argument, *goodness* to the moral argument, and so on, depending upon the kind of experience which the individual finds most potentially meaningful. But, as Hume and Kant pointed out, there are weaknesses in the empirical approach unless it is supplemented with that which goes beyond basic perception. To make sense of perception one must appeal to experience that is broader than sensory perception. Thus any satisfactory approach to God will be a combination of the rationalistic and empirical regardless of the focus of attention.

This study utilizes the soteriological approach. Methodologically, it is not necessarily superior to any other combination of the empirical and rational. It begins, as is obvious from previous chapters, with the experience of salvation and attempts to account for that basic experience by appealing to that which is beyond sensory experience. Just as the physicist posits the subsensory world of his discipline, so the philosopher of religion may posit the supersensory (levels of divinity and deity) in order to account for the empirical world of his discipline.

Just as the nuclear physicist must cultivate a special quality of awareness to make sense of the electron, proton, meson, and other subatomic realities, so also the theologian must develop a special awareness or unique state of being in order to make sense of God. Just as one can refine his thinking and redefine his world, so also he can cultivate peculiar sensibilities. We see with our eyes, but we also *look*. We hear with our ears, but we also *listen*. We "prehend" with our whole being, but we also "*behold*." The soteriological approach will explore the capacity for beholding and attempt to define that which is beheld as God.

Agent and Grace as Clues to God. In the second chapter we suggested that the quest for salvation is a clue to understanding man in every place and time, individually and socially. Salvation was interpreted as creative well-being which included both a disciplined life orientation and momentary intense "beholdings" that may be overwhelming. Salvation as disciplined life orientation involved a creative ordering of the environment, a process that often encountered a resistant, obstructive, or destructive element. Thus, in many instances there was recognized need for an assisting *agent*. At the same time there are many moments of creative well-being that seem independent of any effort and hence surprise one as a gift of *Grace*.

In a life of creative well-being both agent and Grace are clues to God. The agent as *agent* is instrumental to the more meaningful life and hence is special environment. But in the *christ*ian experience of salvation the christ is more than cooperating environment; the christ may take a beneficial initiative which in effect not only establishes an appropriate environment but also is agency to a quality of awareness that beholds a Beyond, which in turn feels incarnated in the beholding. There is an assurance of a supersensory reality which seems to escape immediate perceptive imagery, but the denial of which offends the total experience. Thus any rational and dispassionate analysis of the experience of salvation must posit a *more* that is essential. In a sense one could say that the agent is a clue to Grace.

Grace is also a clue to God. The second chapter indicated that both risk and luck were involved in the experience of salvation, that salvation could not be interpreted merely as the results of effort, sacrificial intrigue, or of chance; in part, it is a "gift of Grace." It is essential at this point to explain what is meant by "Grace." In traditional Christian theology, Grace refers "to the free and unmerited act through which God restores his estranged creatures to himself."[42] It is used here without the traditional connotations of sin and estrangement because these notions imply that man has deliberately alienated himself from God. In this study, as we will see, man's relation with God is more like "encountering a stranger" than in "reconciling an estrangement." Grace is used here in a much narrower sense because it does suggest an act of God (gift) that is to some extent independent of merit. Hence, the gift does not necessarily imply benevolence on the part of the giver or worthiness on the part of the recipient. By the same token it does not follow that all salvation is totally unrelated to effort. We have seen that creative ordering of the environment is often essential to salvation and that the appropriate psychological attitude is part of that creative ordering. Much basic enjoyment in life can be won through direct effort, but there remains a ratio that must be defined as "gift." "Grace" refers to this restricted area that has special significance.

Behind every gift there is some kind of giver. The troubling question now is whether or not there are any strings attached that will give us additional information about the identity of the giver. The gift itself may be something of a clue.

God as Abstract Noun and Proper Name. The discussion here must keep in mind that in Christian theology the word "God" has a double reference. It may be used as "an abstract noun for deity" or as a "proper name."[43] To speak of God in the former sense is to identify an objective reality that is a meaningful part of the nature of things. The particular conception of deity propounded will depend upon the specific theologian or philosopher of religion involved; but, regardless of the notion suggested, God in this sense refers to some identifiable being whose nature and function can be discussed dispassionately and independently of one's own religious convictions. Since the term has been used through the ages to refer to any number of differing notions, it may be said to be an "abstract noun for deity." This is the God of the treatise, of metaphysics and cosmology, the God of the classroom.

Speaking of God as a "proper name" is quite different. In this case one is speaking of the God of personal experience, of a *Thou* with whom one may have a personal encounter, One who has *revealed* himself through his initiative. This is the God of scripture, of testimony, of worship and chapel. Whereas the adequacy of the notion of God of the metaphysical treatise depends upon inclusive and detailed description in a system as a whole, the adequacy or "proof" of the God of worship depends upon the clarity and power of the revelation and encounter. The former God lends himself to man's rational analysis and description; the latter God grasps man through an ineffable beholding.

Relating God as "abstract noun" and as "proper name" has been one of the most difficult and persistent problems in the history of religion. Each can be understood in such a way that any reconciliation of the two is impossible. For example, as abstract noun, God may be interpreted as so remote and impersonal that any kind of intimate encounter is impossible. In such a case God is so transcendent that his immanence is out of the question. But, on the other hand, the God who is addressed in prayer, God as proper name, is so mysterious, so overwhelming, so ineffable, so totally incomprehensible that any attempts to articulate the nature of the Person are doomed from the outset. In terms of these extreme interpretations no adequate relationship is possible.

But one need not think only in terms of these extremes. It is possible to modify the understanding of God as abstract noun and as proper name so that the dichotomy can be bridged. In the thought of Alfred North Whitehead, God seems to begin as abstract noun, but before the discussion is completed Whitehead shows how the total reality that is God includes an "initial aim" for every "actual entity." God is not only transcendent in that he stands under all that is, he is also as immanent as our noblest aspirations. Whitehead has discussed the nature of God, the nature of the world, and the intimate relations between them in such detail as to show how the chasm between abstract noun and personal name is overcome. The clue comes in his suggesting that the initial phase of the subjective aim of every actual entity comes from God. In more common terminology this means that God touches man's life by holding before him the lure for salvation. One can hardly complete an alert reading of Whitehead without encountering his God as a *Thou.* This is a Being that one can and does address in prayer because the beauty of the system of thought is so overwhelming. When one permits this abstract noun to become a proper name he discovers, with Whitehead, a "tender care that nothing be lost."[44]

Once God is experienced as proper name, there is no returning simply to abstract noun. Once God is encountered as a *Thou,* all of reality takes on a new dimension of meaning when the attention is drawn to God. In moments of reverie one might try to analyze and comprehend the dimensions of such encounters, but there is always a vast area that remains unavailable and unexplored. Descriptive detail can relate the phenomenological aspects of the event but the total depth cannot be understood, much less communicated. The elements of wonder and ecstasy forever escape our most diligent attempts to articulate the fulfillment of the event, and though our gifts of expression may begin to describe the environment of the event, we never lose full sight of the proper name center, the nucleus of which seems to remain forever hidden.

Another fact must be acknowledged at this point. While there are many who utilize the notion of God as abstract noun and many others who experience God as proper name, there are many others who claim to have no need for either of these. Like Laplace, in his answer to Napoleon's question about God, there are those who can think of reality with sufficient inclusiveness and coherence to satisfy their curious minds without any formulation of or concern for a notion of God. By the same token, there are many who have never had an encounter with God as a *Thou* but insist nonetheless that their lives are rich and fulfilling. One must acknowledge such a variety of attitudes that one can be *saved* without knowledge of God (as I interpret God) or of worship (as I interpret worship) just as one can live meaningfully without an assurance of a transcendent heaven, or personal survival in some life after death, or even in inevitable progress in the generations to follow on earth. But it is easy to understand how those who have had such encounters or hold such beliefs would feel that these encounters and beliefs would add immeasurably to the lives of those who have not.

In secular christian salvation God can be spoken of in terms of both abstract noun and proper name. As abstract noun, God is the total environment that is relevant to salvation, the totality of reality that is involved in the experience of salvation. Since we have made the experience of salvation central, such a reference implies a close connection with the notion of God as proper name. As suggested earlier, salvation includes both the basic durational orientation of life as well as the intense moments of mystic awareness. Generally speaking, the basic durational orientation of life can relate to God as abstract noun while the moments of mystic awareness or "beholding" can relate to god as proper name. In the moments of "beholding," there is an encounter in an environment that is intensely personalized even though it escapes articulation. Nonetheless, the encounter with a *Thou* is ineffably certain. In the pages that follow we will try to show that there need be no sharp distinction between God as abstract noun and God as proper name. Through the environment that is christ, or church, or community, the problem of relating these two modes of deity is largely overcome.

3. GOD AND THE SECULAR CHRISTS

The transition from God as abstract noun to God as proper name can be illustrated through the notion and experience of "christ," whether in the one-way or the two-way form. Thus it is impossible to overemphasize the vital relation between God and the secular christs in a secular christian salvation. Several specific points should make this relation clear: the transition from abstract noun to proper name in the christ experience, the explanation of the notion of God as "in christ," and the notion of christ as "divine."

Christ: From Abstract Noun to Proper Name. Throughout history there have been numerous times when man has experienced the transition from abstract noun to proper name. This transition can be illustrated through the notion of christ as we have defined the term. We suggested earlier that specific instances can be found in the Old Testament, the other world religions, and in the contemporary world. The most notable example for the ancient Western world is that of the New Testament, Jesus of Nazareth. For many years the people of his time and place had been expecting "messiah" or "christ." Undoubtedly, for most of them this was largely "abstract noun" as there was a wide variety of notions of who or what "messiah" would be. Then, as the kerygma of the New Testament testifies, a small band of people encountered a man who transformed their lives to such an extent that they proclaimed him "christ," and an abstract noun (christ) became incarnate in a proper name (Jesus). Anyone who could do anything like that is surely no ordinary man. Small wonder that new symbols, myths, and legends appeared to begin the formation of a new scriptural tradition. How could man describe adequately an experience so overwhelming?

God as "in Christ": Immanent, Secular, and Incarnate. If one may define God in the mode of abstract noun as the total environment that is relevant to salvation, and if one can use the term "christ" to refer to any personal agent in salvation, it naturally follows that God is "in christ." God refers to the larger and more general total environment while christ refers to the more specific and special personal environment.

God is also "in christ" in the mode of proper name, though it is expressed differently. When fundamental but frustrated hopes find their fulfillment through a specific agency, the agent represents more than what is observed through the senses. The role is symbolic of a reality that escapes immediate perception. In and through the christian experience one beholds an ineffable reality that is behind and beyond the immediate moment and place. Just as the role of the agent represents the larger context of the company agency, so also the christian experience lays hold of a Behind and Beyond that remains hidden, a vast potentiality, a reservoir of Grace—God. Thus in the mode of proper name we can speak of God as "in christ."

In a carefully qualified sense one could maintain that another way of distinguishing the two modes of deity is through the use of the terms "transcendence" and "immanence." When applied to God, transcendence refers to God's being as separate from the world, as being prior to it or exalted beyond it. It connotes detachment, lack of concern, even impersonality. Hence, it would seem to apply to God in the mode of abstract noun. In contrast, immanence suggests nearness or indwellingness, God's involvement in the world, his intimate concern and providential care. Thus immanence suggests the mode of proper name.

In the experience of secular christian salvation God is beheld as both immanent and transcendent. The notion of God as "in christ" suggests the intimate involvement of God in the christ function. In the christ event, God is beheld as inexpressibly near, as immanent. But there is another aspect of the christ event that requires the notion of transcendence. It is an occasion that points beyond itself. Just as there is assurance of Presence, so also there is equal confidence of a vastness, a depth and distance the full dimension of which escapes our keenest contemplation. To attempt to express the overwhelming mystery, the ineffable awe that leaves one lost in wonder and ecstasy, one must use a term like "transcendence." Clearly, the christ experience reveals a reality behind and beyond itself for which it is agent, and it is the revelatory quality that helps to distinguish "christ" from "God."

To speak of God as *secular* in christ is another way of referring to the immanence of God. But the point assumes added power when one refers to christ as a secularizer of God in the sense that a christ often avails God to specific time and place. There are many instances in the personal world when a christ "catalyst" avails the creative presence of God which otherwise would have remained inaccessible. There are times when "God has no hands but our hands, no feet but ours." The more one ponders the dependency of God upon christ in the personal world the more one realizes the significance of christ as a secularizer of God.

To express the full force of the intimate relation between God and christ as here defined one can speak of God as *incarnate* in christ. This does not mean that God literally becomes flesh, as earlier centuries have understood the theological notion of the incarnation. Rather, it refers to that christian event in which God becomes as immediate and real as one can experience or behold, an "I-Thou" encounter. While the christ experience invariably points beyond itself, there is a temporal empirical aspect in which the agent and the agency are superimposed as one and the same, an incarnation. It has to do, not with the nonfleshly becoming flesh, but rather with degrees of proximity and clarity. These are clear avenues for the divine.

Christ as Divine. It appears that man has always been both intrigued and puzzled in his attempts to relate the human and the divine. In ancient Egypt, Babylonia, and Greece the pharaohs and the emperors were in some cases looked upon as gods, an obvious overlapping of these categories. Other religious traditions have tried to establish and maintain a marked distinction, but without success. While Judaism has emphasized the oneness of God and the separation of God and man, it has utilized the notions of "sons of God," "Son of God," "anointed one," and other such titles in which the distinction is obviously not so distant or distinct. Traditional Christianity has emphasized the chasm between man the fallen sinner and the Triune God eternal in the heavens. And yet, one of the Persons of the Triune God depends upon an interpretation of Jesus that bridges the gap, very God and very man. One must conclude that no inflexible distinctions can be made in the Western religious traditions.

In this study the notion of the divine has nothing to do with the old mythological pattern, with neither transcendent distance nor substance. Rather, it has to do with function, with the degree of relevance to salvation. Just as salvation is a matter of degree, so divinity is a matter of degree. It means standing in special relation to or proximity with God. Any agent who facilitates salvation is behaving in God's and our behalf. Such significant soteriological action may be referred to as "divine," and any agent who can be identified as essential or instrumental to the process is to that extent divine.

4. GOD AND THE SECULAR CHURCH

The discussion of the secular church in salvation attempted to show the close relationship between the notion of "christ" and the notion of "church." The preceding section attempted to establish the intimate relationship between God and christ. With those two discussions in mind it follows that there is a similar functional affinity between God and the church. This section will illustrate this relation by exploring God as immanent and transcendent in the church, God in the life of the church, and the church as divine.

God as Immanent and Transcendent in the Church. In the discussion of God as immanent and secular in christ we suggested that the christ event served as an occasion for God to become more immediately available to a specific time and place. The same seems to follow in the case of the church, though on the social level. Just as there is an assurance of God as "proper name" through the christ event at the individual or personal level, so also there is a corporate assurance of the presence of God in the church event at the social level. Thus, two points are being stressed here. The first is the feeling of confidence in the presence of God, as emphasized also in the case of God as immanent in christ, the assurance of the actual involvement of God on a "proper name" basis. The second is the fact of the experience at the social level. To be able to communicate meaningfully about an experience of God at the social level is to escape some of the limitations of the notion of the subjectivity of God. If a group can share a common experience and discuss it dispassionately and in detail, it helps each member of the group to feel more certain that the importance of the experience is more than a mere figment of the individual's imagination. Indeed, to establish an environment that is understood by the group as common to the group is to go far toward objectivity. In any case, the church is an avenue for the revelation of the otherwise hidden God at the social level of being.

Although God is acknowledged as present and involved in the salvation experience at the church level, God is also experienced as Beyond. To move from the one-way christ relation to the many-way christ event is to make a significant transition from "my God" to "our God." Not only does this move in the direction from subjectivity to objectivity, it also provides empirical awareness of another dimension of deity, the very dimension that is essential to the notion of transcendence. Careful empirical analysis shows that every experience points beyond itself. The problem arises in attempting to describe and name the Beyond. But when the Beyond is *beheld* as both essential in and transcendental to the experience of salvation at the christ and church levels, we choose to name it "God." Whether or not this naming is legitimate or convincing must depend upon the study as a whole. But the experience of God as both abstract noun and proper name hints that there are vast areas of potentiality yet unexplored. Indeed, there seems to be no apparent limitation to the transcendence of God. To deny such a dimension is to fail to deal adequately with the experience of salvation, especially at the church level.

God in the Life of the Secular Church. The primary function of the secular christian church is its service of worship. For this reason, we have referred to worship as the life of the church. Worship refers to any symbolic church behavior which anticipates or expresses salvation. As anticipatory or expectant, worship invites and encourages the experience of the presence of God. As expressive, it acknowledges an experience of the presence of God. As anticipatory, it is deliberate and dedicated, as well as being charged with feeling. As expressive, it is kerygmatic, proclaiming or testifying to an event that has happened. Thus the life of a secular christian church is clearly oriented around its worship service, and it is in the service of worship that God is most expected and evident at the social level. God provides the worship a locus and goal which itself in turn provides the best avenue for the mystery of Grace to take place. Hence, the temple as the sanctuary for worship is the sacred laboratory for experimenting with God and the process of salvation. To save us, the church must know our need, and this is possible only to the extent that we honestly reveal it; but when the church functions as it should, as a body of christs, worship in general and prayer in particular demonstrate the presence and power of God.

The Secular Church as Divine. In the discussion of Christ as divine we suggested that we were using the term "divine" to mean "standing in special relation to or proximity with God." Since christ refers to a personal agent in salvation, and since any special agent in salvation is acting in both God's and our behalf, this agent (christ) can be considered to be divine. Since the church is to function at the social level in the same way as the christ functions at the individual or personal level, it would follow that it is clearly acting in a special way in God's and our behalf, and thus can be said to be divine. It is important to emphasize, however, that although the church is *of* God, it is *not* to be identified *as* God. In the mode of abstract noun, God can be defined as the total environment of salvation. In the same form, the church can be seen as a part of that total environment. But God is transcendent to the church both in the mode of abstract noun and in the mode of proper name. Moreover, there is a larger community that may also function in a special soteriological capacity. Although clearly very special, the church is not God because it is not ultimate. To consider it such is to fall into idolatry. But it may, nonetheless, be regarded as divine.

5. GOD AND THE SECULAR COMMUNITY

While the relationships between God and christ and God and the church are natural enough in the common mind, the relationship between God and the community is more controversial and therefore needs careful examination. As it is conceived in this study, the relation will soon be evident when we recall that the church is clearly a part of a larger community both through its relations with other churches and through its relations with other institutions. If we recall also that in the mode of abstract noun we used the term "God" to refer to the "total environment that is relevant to salvation," it would follow that there is a relation between God and the community.

God in the Community Institutions. A community is a more or less localized and unified center of social or institutionalized activities. As suggested earlier, the various institutions are not to be thought of as autonomous or self-sufficient. Each requires a larger cultural environment in terms of which it can fulfill its specific needs. Hence, it was argued that the community itself has a soteriological function. The title of the fifth chapter, "The Secular Community as Christian," as well as the topics of the sections of the chapter, "Fulfillment in Employment" and "Re-creation Through Leisure," intended to convey this very thesis. In speaking of the community as christian we give the clue to understanding God's relation to it. It is the community's functioning in a soteriological capacity that makes the relevance of God most evident.

The relation of God and the secular community can be illustrated with each of the institutions that have been identified as having a special function in the soteriological process. Insofar as the home and family, the school, employment, leisure, and government contribute uniquely to the abundant life, they are avenues of immanence and transcendence for God in the modes of abstract noun and proper name. It is in the unique contribution of each of the institutions that the relevance of God is most apparent.

Relating God to each of the institutions in the secular community helps to emphasize the importance of each. To see the relation of God to the home and family is to sanctify this institution of man. To see the relation of God to the school should alert the larger community all the more to the needs and potentialities of this often neglected institution. To identify the role of God in both vocation and vacation is to add dimensions of meaning to our daily life. In sum, to interpret each institution as an avenue of salvation—as it clearly is—is to sensitize us anew to the vast soteriological resources that often largely escape us.

God and the Larger Realities. The discussion cannot stop at the level of the community or state because there are larger realities that shape the destiny of states. We saw earlier that the more responsible states of our time are discovering that both domestic and foreign policies are influenced to a great extent by the attitudes of citizens of other states as well as the citizens of the state in question. This means that loyalties and authorities are being established which clearly extend beyond the geographical boundaries of any individual particular state. The same problem that intrigues us in connection with lower and less complex levels of reality reappears here. Just as the cell cannot be understood accurately and adequately apart from the organism of which it is a part, so the individual state today cannot be understood apart from a larger international scene of which it is aware and with which it is expected to function. With current developments in communications and transportation, the military dangers that are clearly evident, and the military destruction of which man is capable, the present political situation demands that the various sovereign states acknowledge an international responsibility and, if necessary, a national submission to an international authority designed to serve the purposes of the earth as a whole. It may well be that the citizens of earth may be forced to deal with problems of interplanetary negotiation before they have established an effective international organization. In any case, there are larger realities that fashion the destiny of nations. With this introduction, we turn to a brief discussion of God and nature and God and history.

6. GOD AND NATURE

The relationship between God and nature has been a major problem for many centuries and a significant body of literature has appeared on this theme. Our discussion will have to be limited to a few selected topics that are central to the thesis of this study, namely, the realm of nature as environment for salvation, God as immanent in and transcendent to nature, nature as divine and demonic, and God and natural evil.

The Realm of Nature as Environment for Salvation. There are two approaches to the realm of nature that are relevant here. In the objective one, nature refers to the objects or phenomena known through the senses, to the areas that are investigated by the natural sciences, of matter and energy in whatever form or amount they may appear. Nature is the sum total of everything in time and space, the so-called physical universe in its entirety. In the romantic approach, nature refers to the vast expanse of earth and heaven, to a full moon on an ebbing tide, to jagged mountain peaks that pierce the sky and rip the clouds in the wind, to chirping cricket and katydid, to stately spruce and pine silhouetted against a twilight sky, to the sun's beams reflected in the crystal dew, to eagle's wings and dancing fern, to buzzing bee and blooming meadow, to gurgling brook and quiet lake—to the whole panorama of the seasons and the stars.

To speak of nature in a romantic way is to notice its great value for the enriched life. At one point or another in their lives most people come into a natural environment of such inexpressible beauty that the time and place leave an indelible impression on the memory that later enriches each moment of recall. To see "grass" we need Carl Sandburg more than spectacles. Who does not covet the poetic acuity of Robert Frost when he watches the "woods fill up with snow"?

In addition to the spontaneous discovery of natural beauty that takes the breath, there is a cooperative orderliness available to man's imagination in nature making possible his creating lovely gardens of vegetables and flowers that nourish both body and spirit. He can husband the forests and the mountains, harness the streams, irrigate the desert to make it flower, and turn the earth into a paradise. Nature abounds in joyous surprises and cooperative responses until man is left dazzled by its mysterious wonders. Surely life would be immeasurably impoverished were it not for both the surprising and the predictable beauty in nature.

God as Immanent in and Transcendent to Nature. God's immanence in nature can be shown by definition and by experience. On the one hand, if we define God as the total environment that is relevant to salvation and then, on the other hand, show that nature is an avenue for salvation, it follows that one can argue that God is immanent in nature. Moreover, the definition is borne out in firsthand experience. The fact is that nature does serve as an environment for beholding God; it provides a locus in which God in the mode of abstract noun becomes God in the mode of proper name. Thus God is immanent in both modes.

Each mode also speaks to God's transcendence, both by experience and by definition. To experience God as proper name in the realm of nature is to behold a Presence in the midst of a Beyond, the immediate in terms of something that is essentially hidden. The encounter with the *known* reveals a depth and breadth of an *unknown* with a haunting quality that never fully escapes us. For this reason we must acknowledge that God cannot ever be entirely immediate. We have seen earlier how the church and the community, in similar fashion, provide an environment for the type of experience that posits God's transcendence. Thus it appears that God in the immanence of proper name assumes the transcendence of abstract noun. Hence, a soteriological approach requires both God's immanence in and God's transcendence to nature.

Nature as Divine and Demonic. Following the same logic of earlier discussions, one can argue that there are aspects of nature that are divine. We have seen already that both christ (at the personal level) and church (at the social level) are divine in that they stand in special relation to or proximity with God. As an avenue for salvation at its own level, nature fulfills an identical function and hence can, to that extent, be considered divine. Anyone who has known God in the mode of proper name through the medium of nature will mark the time and place as holy or divine.

But there is another face of nature that must not escape our notice. The romantic and poetic approach should not blind us to the indifference and even ruthlessness of nature. The same calm tide that reflects the moon's full beams at one hour may at another turn turbulent to claim the life of sailor and of ship. The same bright sun that warms the springtime to bring to life the sleepy crocus may in another time and place parch the meadow and lay waste the land. The gentle breeze that cools the sweating brow may too soon turn to hurricane and wreck the palace and the gardens of a lifetime. The fire that warms the hearth may also claim the house. The same mysterious cycle of the seasons bringing exciting springtime planting and bounteous harvest may also bring famine, plague, and flood. The same bed that holds the wonders of love and life may also hold the fevered and the dead. There are times when nature seems ruthless and enraged, bent on destruction, as if under the power of some deranged demon or god gone mad. This part, too, must find a place in our soteriology.

God and Natural Evil. One of the most challenging problems of all time is that of theodicy, that is, the reconciliation of an omni-God with the natural evil that plagues the earth. If God is both all-powerful and all-good, there should be no natural evil. Natural evil does not refer to the misery that can be laid at the door of man—war, pollution, overpopulation, and the like. Rather, it refers to the distress that is part of the nature of things—plague, earthquake, hereditary weaknesses, and the like. If we assume that nature and man were the result of cosmic chance, then we would expect to find the kind of world we do. But if there is a designing Mind and Hand, benevolent, omniscient, omnipotent, and omnipresent, fashioning the starry skies, leaving fingerprints in the Pleiades and the Belt of Orion, willing and controlling the seedtime and the harvest— then how are we to account for the "destruction that wastes at noonday"? Long before and ever since the time of Job men have made eloquent their plea for understanding why the wicked flourish while the righteous perish. Somewhere on the earth every hour someone will face the age-old problem of the meaning of God in the midst of natural tragedy.

In the past, men have usually sought a solution in one of several ways. The orthodox believer is inclined to reaffirm his faith in the omni-God and acknowledge, however reluctantly, that whatever happens is the will of God whether we are able to understand it or not. On the other hand, the more liberal thinker will deny that the tragedy is the will of God and then go on to acknowledge, however reluctantly, that some events happen *in spite of* rather than *because of* the will of God. This means that one cannot think of God as omnipotent, since there are some things God cannot do, namely, prevent the tragedy in question.

Each of these alternative solutions has serious weaknesses. The former, that of the orthodox, denies the evilness of evil by interpreting it as an instrumental good under the guise of the will of God. It assumes a basic faultiness in human judgment in measuring the evilness of evil and in understanding the apparently superrational doings of some supposed deity. This alternative is unsatisfactory because most men are more convinced of the evilness of evil than they are of the existence of the omni-God. Besides, if human judgment is faulty in appraising evil, is it any more trustworthy in affirming good and God? And if man can escape the limitations of human reason through divine revelation, then why is there not some convincing revelation that solves the problem? The latter alternative is better, though not adequate. It attempts to salvage the omni-benevolence of God by compromising the omnipotence of God. Natural evil arises from an aspect of reality that is not yet under the control of God. Whereas the former alternative denies the reliability of human judgment in this area, this one claims far more knowledge of God than is available to human experience. Moreover, there is no evidence that God is making any progress in gaining control of the unruly aspect apart from the efforts of man. Hence, this alternative is also unsatisfactory.

An adequate solution to the problem of God and natural evil requires a new orientation. This new orientation requires not only new notions of God and nature, it also depends upon a new notion of God and history. Evil is as dependent upon the notion of history as it is upon the notion of nature. Hence, we delay further discussion of this specific problem until we have dealt with "God and History."

7. GOD AND HISTORY

The relationship between God and history has been central to the development of the Judeo-Christian tradition. The earliest records claim that God influenced the lives of the patriarchs, led the sons of Jacob out of Egyptian bondage under the leadership of Moses, arranged that his prophet anoint David to be king of Israel and Judah, punished both Israel and Judah in their respective political demises, spoke to Jeremiah through a new covenant, directed Cyrus and the edict of liberation, guided Ezra and Nehemiah in the restoration of the Hebrew homeland, and acted climactically through the incarnation of his Word in Jesus of Nazareth. Each phase of the historical development of the tradition found in itself more conclusive evidence of God's continued involvement in history.

The relationship between God and history is no less central in the thesis of this study. To make this clear we will indicate why we must move from nature to history, what is meant by history, and how it can be interpreted as an avenue of salvation, the way in which God is both immanent in and transcendent to history, and finally, the extent to which one can speak of history without utilizing the notion of God as defined here.

From Nature to History. Strange as it may sound at first, the need for the transition from nature to history can be shown most clearly by distinguishing the old and the new interpretations of matter. The old notion of matter, following the lines of common sense, assumed that everything was reducible to tiny particles called atoms. It was thought that the atoms were both imperishable and unchangeable and that everything in nature was ultimately reducible to the structure and behavior of atoms. Their substance was believed to be independent of either their spatial or temporal relationships. In other words, the atoms were what they were regardless of their environment, the old substance orientation.

As the knowledge of man increased the old theory of matter became less and less satisfactory. There were a number of questions that it was unable to answer. For example, how is one to account for change? If the atoms themselves are unaffected by the environment, there must be some external force that plays upon them to relate them in various ways. But if all reality is made of atoms, then this power must also be made of atoms. How is one to account for the transfer of motion from one atom to another? Even more problematic, how is one to understand the relationship between the atoms? Is that atomic too? Finally, how is anyone to account for anything that is genuinely novel? Geology and biology demonstrate genuine evolutionary development among and within the various species. Modern physics dealt the final blow when it advanced to the point of splitting the atom. Clearly, the old theory of matter had to be replaced.

A new theory of matter made significant advances in that it was able to explain more systematically and completely a larger part of man's known world. Modern physics has demonstrated that there are subatomic realities, electrons, protons, neutrons, and so on. Basic to the transition from atomic to subatomic is the realization that these realms have nothing in common. The laws that apply to the atomic level do not apply to the subatomic realm. At the subatomic level the notion of matter is replaced with energy. What was once thought to be a lump of inert stuff has suddenly become something that is totally active, and its activity is such as to require new conceptions of space and time. One cannot locate a subatomic reality in space or time because the energy involved will not coordinate with the commonsense notions of space and time in the sensory world. Moreover, what the subatomic realities *are* depends entirely upon what they *do*, and what they do depends upon their environment. In other words, the "nature" of the subatomic realities depends upon a vast system of interrelationships, just the opposite of what was formerly assumed about the atoms, and the horizons of the environments that constitute the subatomic realities are very problematic. As indicated earlier, this has meant a basic shift in understanding the nature of things —from substance to function.

The new theory of matter has some very significant implications for our present study in that it has taught us a more reliable method for approaching *superatomic* realities. To understand any aspect of reality one must know it in the appropriate spatial and temporal terms. Subatomic particles move at such speeds that to describe them in terms of an instant in space is to fail to observe them accurately. If one is to understand a cell accurately, he must see it in terms of its own spatial and temporal function. To understand man we must observe his patterns of behavior. As R. G. Collingwood has pointed out, in terms of an *instant* there is no difference between a body that is dead and a body that is alive.[45] The difference is evident only when the observation includes the appropriate conditions and durations of behavior. The same can be said for cultures and civilizations. From all this it is surely obvious that a reliable understanding of any aspect of nature depends upon an appropriate temporal dimension, that is, history.

History as an Avenue of Salvation. The study of history has become so extensive and detailed that a wide variety of definitions is now possible. It can be argued that history deals with the past, the present, or the future. In common usage history refers to the record of *past* events, especially those events which are relevant to the development of human affairs. Without some such limitation the sciences of paleontology and paleobotany would be branches of history rather than branches of geology and botany respectively. Or, secondly, history may be concerned with the *present* inasmuch as it is being shaped by the past. In this sense, history is the present interpretation of past events insofar as they are relevant to the current scene.[46] Some historians would insist that the focus of interest is still the past rather than the present. Thirdly, one could argue that history is concerned with the *future*. No one would deny the influence of the past on the present or of the present on the future. Every historian is selective of events in terms of his point of view. The same norms that operate in the selection of events as significant in and constitutive of the historical process will also feature in the attempt to understand the goal of history. Thus the historian is legitimately concerned about the future and could well argue that it is the future that justifies the study of history if anything does.

For our present purposes, history should be understood as that temporal sequence of events which, along with nature (the spatial distribution of events), accounts for present events being what they are. This does not mean that nature and history constitute the totality of reality. There must be a place for God and man. Nor does it mean that either nature or history can be understood accurately in isolation from the other. A reliable interpretation of either requires a consideration of the other. But for purposes of introductory simplicity, we attempt to identify some aspects of a definition of history in isolation from nature.

To summarize, history here refers to that temporal sequence of events in the past which gives shape and meaning to a present focus of interest. To say this is to identify several elementary but fundamental aspects of history. First, it is a *sequence* of events. To make sense as history every fact or event must be seen as a part of a chronological chain where temporal relations can be observed. Secondly, as a sequence it must be *orderly*, at least in a chronological sense. Some facts or events must be seen as earlier and some as later, with some discernible causal factor at work in the evolutionary process. Thirdly, the temporal sequence roots in the *past*. This is not to deny that the present influences the past as much as the past influences the present. But as far as history is concerned the temporal location of the sequence of events is more past than present. Finally, there is the importance of the *focus of interest*. The significance of any past event depends upon the historian's focus of interest. One does not write a history of reality; one may attempt a history of America or a history of transportation or of dueling. In any case there is a focus of interest that may or may not involve the contemporary scene.

It can now be shown how history can be interpreted as an avenue of salvation, whether salvation is thought of in its momentary and intense form or in its developing and durational form. In both of these forms there is a "given" element, as there is in any and all experience. History is one aspect of the given (along with nature, God, and man). In the case of the developing and durational aspect of salvation, history is the temporal background in terms of which the all-important transition from instrumental to intrinsic and from intrinsic to instrumental value is made. The chronological background that is essential to creative well-being is illustrative of the definition of history. In the case of the momentary and intense experience of salvation the importance of history is less obvious because this aspect of salvation often involves an element of surprise. However, more careful examination usually discovers some significant historical preparation. The moments of greatest illumination usually come to those who have spent years in preparatory meditation.

As given, history can facilitate or obstruct the nobler life. Any sequence of events may work for good or ill just as any spatial distribution of events (nature) may do the same. The negative aspects of both history and nature will be considered later. Here the emphasis is on the positive and constructive, and from that point of view it can be concluded that insofar as history is instrumental to the experience of an abundant life, it is an avenue of salvation.

God as Immanent in and Transcendent to History. To the extent that history serves as a medium for salvation in both its momentary and durational forms, and to the extent that these forms are related to the experience of God in either the mode of abstract noun or proper name, to that extent it can be shown that God is both immanent in and transcendent to history. History is usually significant in the experience of salvation as intense and momentary, and the best illustration of such an experience is an encounter with God in the mode of proper name. No experience can be more *historic* than this. If such an encounter with God involves both immanence and transcendence in the events of christ, church, and nature, it would do so with history as well. Thus, if the logic applied in the earlier arguments is sound, its relevance here needs only to be mentioned in passing.

History Without God? To argue that God is transcendent to both nature and history is *not* to suggest that neither has a legitimate realm of its own. Such an argument would mean that all academic disciplines are branches of theology. Actually, both nature and history involve questions and problems which, for adequate answers, must ignore not only God but each other. For any systematic discipline to establish itself, it must focus its interest and thus limit its scope. The history of science shows clearly that we had to "disenchant the forest" in order to understand the forest in terms of itself. For the study of medicine to advance scientifically, we had to eliminate the notion of demons as the cause of disease. We have seen earlier that there are various realms of reality with modes of behavior that are peculiar to themselves. It is often true that the laws of one cannot be used for the understanding of the other. The same is surely true of both nature and history. Hence, it is necessary to assume in an introductory study of nature or history that one need not introduce "supernature" or "superhistory" as a principle of explanation.

On the other hand, this is not to argue that there is no interconnection between the various realms. The farther a science advances the more it discovers the relevance of other areas or levels of reality that were earlier thought to have been irrelevant. Whereas the scientists once spoke of, say, astronomy, physics, biology, and chemistry, now they speak of astrophysics, biochemistry, and so on. Thus, whether or not history can be understood accurately without utilizing a notion of God depends entirely upon the definition of history, the focus of interest, the scope of the problem, *and* the specific understanding of God. Laplace, as a scientist, could inform Napoleon that he had no need for the God hypothesis, but Whitehead has developed a cosmology that shows the relevance of God to any and every aspect of reality. Each is correct in his own frame of reference. To develop a science we had to disenchant the forest; to develop a religion we must reenchant the temple. In a soteriological study the roles of nature, history, and God are so intertwined that an adequate examination of any one must include the relations of all three.

8. GOD AND SALVATION

Our use of the term "salvation" requires that we understand the close relationships between nature, history, and God. We have already explained the need for moving from nature to history in order to have an accurate and adequate understanding of nature. It needs also to be pointed out that the same is true in reverse because it is just as true to say that history is dependent on nature as to say that nature is dependent on history. For introductory studies in each of these areas, some distinctions must be made, but for our present purposes we need to emphasize the interdependence among them. Those significant events which shape the life and destiny of man—whether wars, earthquakes, revolutionary inventions, or volcanic eruptions—are always a combination of both nature and history as we have defined these terms.

Salvation events are always a union of nature and history, space and time, substance and function. We have argued that the salvation event usually requires some diligent and disciplined orientation of the environment. When abandonment to the creative process at work in nature and history is rewarded, sometimes as if by surprise, it seems that all the teleological propensities of both nature and history have come to majestic and mysterious focus and fulfillment in the moments of edification or rapture. Once man has come to see the cooperative creative powers in both nature and history he may utilize them in making his paradise. The creative powers that are immanent in both nature and history seem also to transcend both. This relevant environment we have dared to call God. Hence the intimate internal relations between nature, history, and God. In this concluding section we will attempt to illustrate the significance of these relations insofar as they are relevant to some of the most troublesome themes in modern philosophy of religion.

From God to Salvation. The basic approach of this study has been to move from the experience of salvation to God. The importance of this soteriological approach to the study of philosophy of religion must not be forgotten. But once the transition has been made one ought also to recognize the relevance of the transition from God to salvation. Careful study of nature, history, and God seems to suggest that there are times when the Transcendental takes the initiative in the salvation process. Whitehead has advocated eloquently that God is to be credited with the initial phase of the subjective aim of every actual entity's lure for satisfaction. It requires an actual entity of a very high order to recognize the source of the lure, but once that Source is recognized and acknowledged the whole process of salvation assumes a transcendental glow. It is through the experience of salvation that we come to know God, and once that Source is known as God, we are the better able to identify and honor the lure to satisfaction. Thus, in the final analysis, salvation is largely a gift of Grace.

Salvation from Evil. To argue that God may assume the initiative at any point in the process of salvation is to involve God in a special way in salvation from evil. Evil has been defined as anything that obstructs or destroys the salvation process or event. If God is credited with the capacity of assuming the initiative at any point, no discussion of salvation from evil is complete without specific reference to God's initiative. The question that arises immediately in the mind of the traditional Christian is, Why doesn't God assume sufficient initiative to remove all evil in one grand sweep? And the answer of the traditional Christian usually involves man's inability to understand the inscrutable and mysterious workings of God. Given keener insight, man would recognize that in the long range of things the events which appear evil in this life will be understood in the next life as part of God's eternal plan.

From the point of view of this study such an answer is simply inadequate. For one thing, it assumes notions of God, nature, and history that are unreliable. It assumes that God controls both nature and history by fiat and from a distance, that every event is some expression of his will independent of nature and history, and that at any moment he could enter into nature and history to achieve any specific purpose in his larger plan, even though it may be contrary to both nature and history. This leads directly to the problem of evil because man is unable to understand why God doesn't change things for the better. The first step in the solution of the problem of evil is the recognition of the need for a new interpretation of God, of nature, and of history, as suggested earlier in the chapter. Nature, history, and God are not entities that are operating independently of each other. We have attempted to show some of the interrelations of each of these, emphasizing that both nature and history are interdependent and that God is both immanent in and transcendent to both.

The significance of the distinction between the traditional Christian notions of nature, history, and God on the one hand, and the notions of each of these developed here on the other, are vital to the concern of salvation from evil. In the first place, recognizing the intimate internal interrelations and interdependences, it should be noted that God's initiative is limited to the possibilities available in the whole process of salvation. Order is essential to any creative process, and the necessity of order naturally limits the alternatives. Hence, order is a limiting as well as a freeing factor. God's initiative is further limited by the character of the various realities with which he must deal in both the natural and the historical aspects. These are highly complex and thus very restricting. Some of these realities are personal and cultural with volitional ambitions of their own. The extent to which peoples and cultures are free to fashion their own destiny is another limiting factor.

Perhaps it follows from this that God *is* doing everything

possible to reduce and eliminate evil from nature, history, and the life of man. In saying this we are not denying the existence of evil. From the beginning we have acknowledged that salvation involves the creative ordering of the environment and that there may be aspects of the environment which resist such creative ordering. "Evil" is the term we use to refer to just those aspects of the environment which in fact resist creative ordering and hence become obstacles to the better life. Some of these have been identified in the preceding paragraph. What we are saying is that both nature and history provide evidence of the immanence and transcendence of God, and that it is reasonable to assume that God is doing everything possible to reduce and eliminate evil in the world.

If this is the case, then it would follow that there is *no* evil for which God can be held accountable. The evil that still persists does so because it cannot, under prevailing circumstances, be remedied in an instant. The world as we know it has not been created *ex nihilo* and in a twinkling. Reality in any meaningful form must be understood in terms of something (nature) and that something will permit only a limited amount of creative ordering at any time in the temporal process (history). It is childish to assume that all can be made beautiful in a moment. If the earlier discussion of God's relation to both nature and history is well founded, it is reasonable to assume that God is doing everything possible to reduce and eliminate evil and that there is then no actual evil for which God is to be charged.

With this understanding of nature, history, and God, man will not expect the impossible either from God or from his fellowmen, and thus he can avoid the kind of despair that results from unanswered prayers or miracles which fail to come. As David Hume pointed out long ago, if God is associated with the orderly process of creative evolution or advance, there cannot be any momentary or arbitrary interruption of the order of nature to achieve some immediate goal that is foreign to that phase of the orderly process itself. To attempt to illustrate the miraculous in this way is but an exhibition of folly. At the same time man discovers that his own noblest efforts may enhance the creative process in the world and thus reduce to a minimum his frustration and disappointment in the face of genuine tragedy.

In conclusion, could it not be suggested that the lure to salvation is itself the best way to overcome evil in the world? Whitehead would have us believe that it is at this very point that God touches our lives most intimately—that he holds before us and all levels of reality the vision of the nobler life at the moment when we are most susceptible. Wieman suggests that the best solution to the problem of evil is total commitment to that reality which can change us as we cannot change ourselves. In other words, the best possible solution to the problem of evil is total commitment to the process of salvation, especially at those times when evil is most apparent.

Salvation from Sin. Through the ages the Christian church has been neurotically preoccupied with sin. By definition, sin is offending God's holy laws as they are revealed in sacred scripture or church doctrine—any action of thought or deed that violates God's will as duly acknowledged by church or scripture. There are, it seems, many different kinds of sin: actual, mortal, venial, sins of omission, and sins of commission. There is even said to be original sin which man somehow inherited from some mischief of Adam in the myth of the Garden of Eden. The foolishness of this was pointed out as early as Jeremiah and Ezekiel (Jer. 31:29–30 and Ezek. 18:1–4) but this seems to have escaped the notice of traditional Christianity. The most reliable definition of sin in the New Testament is found in James 4:17, "Whoever knows what is right to do and fails to do it, for him it is sin." Even this definition, to be useful, can be applied only in cases where it is really possible to do the right.

Criticism of the traditional definitions and attitudes toward sin does not mean that we can dismiss the problem of sin easily. This is one of the most difficult problems with which man has to deal. The brief space that can be allowed to this problem here means that we can identify only some of the more important conditions that are connected with a responsible attitude toward sin.

"Sin" refers to any voluntary or deliberate evil for which

the evildoer can be held accountable. This means that the sinner must be in a position to acknowledge two or more possible ways of thought or action, and these alternatives must be acknowledged as of unequal value. Sin assumes that the sinner deliberately sets aside his commitments of the past, that he chooses short-range benefits over long-range ambitions, that he flouts his own inner sensitivities and integrity for an incoherent and self-destructive path of behavior. The puzzling question is whether anyone would behave in such a fashion unless he was psychologically ill. If he is ill, to what extent does the moral responsibility that is usually associated with sin apply? This question has to be worked out responsibly in Christian theology. This study can touch only briefly some of the important aspects.

Salvation from sin is more problematic than is salvation from evil. Salvation from evil involves accepting certain obstacles as unavoidable. It does not involve individual guilt or personal responsibility. Thus the hurt is not so keen. Sin, on the other hand, involves the inner turmoil and tension associated with feelings of guilt, the depression associated with failure, and the insecurity of not knowing for certain whether the condition can be corrected for good. Thus the initial phases of salvation from sin assume genuine confession and repentance, that is, acknowledgment of having done it and sincere regret for it. But there is no escape that is secure without commitment to the life without sin. At this point the importance of "christ" and "church" becomes apparent. Sin is a kind of sickness for which there seems to be no lasting cure except through a christ and in a church as we have described these functions earlier. These are the very parts of the salvation process designed to cure the sickness that is sin. Every saved sinner knows that christ and the church are of God. There seems to be no other way of salvation from sin.

Heaven and Hell. The otherworldliness of traditional Christianity is most obvious in its interpretations of heaven and hell. Generally speaking, heaven is the distant place where people go after death or after the Judgment Day if their conduct on earth has been such as to merit the endless bliss that heaven affords. Hell refers to that place under the earth that has been created and reserved for those whose deeds on earth have merited the endless suffering this place of damnation entails. Whether or not these general interpretations of traditional Christianity can be considered as scriptural is itself a matter of some dispute, but one fact is perfectly clear. Just as there is a genealogy of God in Biblical literature, so also there is a genealogy of interpretations when it comes to man's condition after death. There was a time when it was assumed that all departed spirits went to Sheol, a place for ghosts, affording neither bliss nor punishment. As religion became more personal and ethical, the notions of heaven and hell were developed to help to make better sense of the unrewarded virtue and unrequited vice of the present world. As the excessive otherworldliness of traditional Christianity passes, so passes the traditional notions of heaven and hell—and none too soon.

But this does not mean that we must strike these words from our vocabulary. Each of them is capable of expressing a new usage within the functional framework of secular christianity. In this study, each of them is to be understood soteriologically. Heaven refers to that state of being when salvation is assured; hell refers to that condition in which the chances for salvation are so jeopardized as to appear unlikely or even impossible. It hardly needs to be added that heaven, thus understood, involves a genuine bliss. It refers to those times in life when one seems totally immune to temptation, indeed, unaware of it. In contrast, alas! is the obvious agony of hell, a torture that is indescribable because it is without apparent hope. But to speak of the ecstasy of heaven and the misery of hell is to speak in terms of extremes. Much of mankind can avoid the extremes of suffering through the soteriological benefits of christ and church.

God and Satan. Just as the notion of God has passed through the generations of polytheism, henotheism, and ethical monotheism, so also the notion of satan has evolved from the early interpretation of being part of the Heavenly Council to the later interpretation of the Prince of Evil, the one who opposes God and lures people into sin. In traditional Christianity, "Satan" is the personification of wickedness, the very "Devil" himself. Like "heaven" and "hell," "Satan" is associated with a prescientific mythology that is now regarded as obsolete. We have just seen that heaven and hell can be reinterpreted in a meaningful way in secular christianity. Now one wonders whether the same can be said for "satan."

One way of approaching a reinterpretation of satan is through the application of the distinction between abstract noun and proper name to the notion of sin. As abstract noun, sin is evil that is deliberately perpetrated. It can be analyzed objectively and from a distance, as in a theological treatise. But sin can also be very concrete and intimate, a firsthand experience with all the guilt and remorse that this entails. Its most demonic form is tempting another person into sin. "Satan" refers to one who deliberately obstructs or destroys the salvation process by luring another into sin, that personal and seductive force which actualizes potential evil in its most agonizing forms. In every such event evil assumes a face and a name.

To clarify what is meant here we can contrast satan with christ. A christ is any personal agent who recognizes another's inability to achieve his desired goal and acts instrumentally to that end. A satan, in contrast, is a personal agent who deliberately manipulates his victim into his nefarious ways, unconcerned about the inner turmoil that is certain to result. Each is an agent; one to evil and the other to good. Since salvation is multifaceted, there are many different christian ways. Evil, too, may assume different forms and thus allow for a variety of satanic activities; but evil is not transcendent as is good. Evil is a derivative notion. Satan may then be contrasted with christ, though not with God. There is no metaphysical or soteriological evil equivalent with God because evil lacks the same degree of transcendence. If this is true, there is reason to hope that man can eliminate the satanic aspects from his life. Since the satanic appears only at the human level, man must assume the initiative in removing it.

To summarize, this chapter has explored the relationships between God and the secular christian life. To do this it suggested that we move "from salvation to God." Careful analysis of the experience of salvation led us to the notion of God as both abstract noun and proper name. But once the notion of God is understood in this detail and is seen to be operative in the various incarnations of christ, church, community, nature, and history, we need to acknowledge a basic initiative on the part of God and thus complete the circle by moving "from God to salvation." In thus moving first from salvation to God, and then second, from God to salvation, we recognize that the salvation enterprise is a cooperative endeavor of internal relationships on the parts of nature, history, God, and man. If this is truly the case, it surely follows that man should exert every effort to organize the larger environment along soteriological lines to achieve the escalating benefits. To a brief description of that challenging and rewarding task we turn in the final chapter of the study.

CHAPTER VII

The Secular
Christian Mission

THE discussion of the preceding chapters seems to find a natural culmination in the notion of the secular christian mission. That is to say, the contents of this chapter follow naturally from what has been said already and illustrate the transition to a natural termination of the entire effort. The careful reader will have detected that the argument so far has been a combination of description and dream, of history and hope. Man's "will to meaning" will become an invitation to existential frustration and despair if it cannot gain realization through the secular christian mission. It is in this sense that we will make the claim that a soteriological approach to the basic issues of life finds its natural culmination in the notion of the secular christian mission as here defined.

1. THE MISSION IDENTIFIED

The first part of the task is identifying the mission, defining it specifically, and showing in what ways it is both christian and secular.

The Specific Mission. "Mission" is the key word in the title of the chapter. The terms "mission" and "missions" have a long and familiar usage in Christian literature. They refer to a special task or purpose for which some individual or group is destined. The usual connotation involves being sent out by God or the church, charged with both responsibility and authority to perform an assigned function. In the case of the Christian

Church this has usually meant preaching the gospel, teaching the Word, healing the sick, proselyting the heathen, and celebrating the appropriate ceremonies, rites, and sacraments. Current criticism of either the means or the goals of the traditional Christian mission must not fail to acknowledge the dedication and the sacrifice that have characterized the entire effort. These sentiments need to be expressed here because the specific mission which faces us now is clearly different from that of traditional Christianity.

From the beginning, one of our basic assumptions has been that the quest for salvation involves the deliberate orientation of the environment in order to increase the probability of fulfillment. We have seen that this applies to every relevant aspect of reality, and we have tried to show this specifically at the levels of the individual, the smaller group, and the larger community. Each of these is preoccupied with specific and appropriate goals which provide the driving power toward the goals and the criteria for evaluating the progress that is made. If one applies this notion to the total environment, he stakes the territory for the mission that we have in mind. The specific mission, then, is establishing that total environment which is most propitious for the process of salvation. This involves arranging the relationships between people, objects, and events in such a way as to increase the chances for satisfaction of aim or purpose. Whereas the earlier chapters have attempted to describe the relationships that make for abundant living, the mission is *establishing* those relations so that the whole soteriological process may get into motion. It must turn on the switch, so to speak, to give the machinery power to function; it must provide the spark for the fire, the pulse for the blood. It is the deliberate and conscientious attempt to transform the dream into reality, to move from the potential to the actual, from the anticipation to the attainment. The mission is to organize the total environment in such a way as to achieve the greatest salvation at every level of being.

The Mission as Christian. The mission is *not* Christian in the traditional sense in that it is not specifically Jesus-oriented, nor is it directed toward one church with one christ. It does not subscribe to the finality of the gospel about Jesus, and it specifically repudiates the notion of one church with one christ. The goal is deliberately more pluralistic. It utilizes all the institutions of man, not just the church.

But in the sense in which we have been using the term, it is obviously christian. All missions, whether religious, political, or military, are teleological in that they are goal-oriented. The success or failure of the mission is measured entirely in terms of the degree to which it achieved its goal. Since the goal here is salvation in both specific and general terms, and since this involves the instrumental agency of orienting the environment in appropriate ways, the mission is clearly christian.

To characterize the mission as christian is to indicate that its purpose is identical to that of the church, the home, the school, the community, and so forth. Only the scope is different. Whereas the institutions of man have more restricted areas of concern, the secular christian mission includes the orientation of every aspect of reality in such a way that it contributes to the enrichment of human life, that it most closely approximates the response of Grace, not only as instrument but further as personal agent. In this sense it attempts to humanize and personify all aspects of the cosmos for their soteriological benefits, from the electron to all nature and from the moment to all history.

Since the secular christian mission is concerned with the total environment in its role as *agent* and its relations with *Grace*, we need to note God's relevance to this mission. Insofar as divine initiative can demonstrate itself in the mission, it is God's most massive attempt to actualize the quest for salvation wherever it might appear and in whatever form. To the extent that the human and the divine initiatives can be coordinated in this missionary enterprise, it is God's and man's most extensive and cooperative effort to fulfill nature and history through the continuous re-creation of each other. Thus, to refer to the christ, the church, and some of the institutions as "incarnations" of God is to acknowledge that they are incarnations in man through the combined efforts of both God and man.

The Mission as Secular. Just as all missions are teleological, so also all missions are space-time oriented. A military mission is probably the most obvious example. In the briefing, every part of the mission is anticipated and defined: the time of departure, the exact route to follow, the specific target, the return trip, and so forth. In describing this mission as secular we mean that it is oriented to this world rather than to some future world. It is here-space and now-time conceived, though not in some arbitrarily isolated or momentary sense as pointed out in the second chapter. As secular, it interprets the present in terms of the remembered past and the anticipated future on the one hand, and on the other, it evaluates both the past and the future in terms of the acknowledged present. Further, as secular, it emphasizes the importance of periodic renewal, of keeping the christian agents both current and relevant in every area of life, and of being mindful of both the demands and the benefits of Grace. All of this is review.

It is also secular in the sense that it must work itself out in a secular age. Although there may still be some individuals and isolated small groups who are otherworldly oriented, the times in which we live are unquestionably secular. Science has long since recognized this; religion is now beginning to do the same.[47] Attempts to delay or compromise the consequences of secularization can be seen in arguments that try to show that earliest Christianity was secular or that the present age is really the fruit of Biblical faith. Usually the claims for "the Biblical sources of secularization" are based upon carefully selected (and carefully neglected) passages that support the supposed thesis. Sometimes the efforts go so far as to draw sharp distinctions between the Hebrew and the Greek, a controversial enterprise at best. In any case, as the second chapter indicated, ours is a secular age and the christian mission is correspondingly secular.

2. SOME OBSTACLES TO THE MISSION

To focus attention upon the secular aspect, having defined the mission as we have, is to become distressingly aware of the enormous gap between life as it is and life as it ought to be.

One cannot but ponder why so little progress is being made. A little reflection reveals that there are formidable obstacles to overcome, obstacles that go beyond the natural environment as resistant, obstructive, and destructive. Some of them are well known to contemporary man.

Disagreement on Ends and Means. Wise and sincere men face one of the most formidable obstacles in what is genuine disagreement on both the goals of the mission and on the means of achieving the goals. All enlightened men agree that all men seek salvation in some form, but not all enlightened men agree on the form that salvation should assume or on whether or not the individual can be given the right to decide what the form of the salvation will be. Even when wise men agree on the goals, there is still danger that they will disagree on the best means of achieving the desired goals. In world diplomacy, East and West agree that man must be free, but they do not agree on the meaning of that freedom or how it is to be established and maintained. In America, North and South agree that *man* should have basic civil rights, but they do not agree (with each other or among themselves) on who is *man enough* to vote. The history of negotiation at every level, both domestic and foreign, reveals the danger that disagreement on either means or ends may delay progress indefinitely. All sane men hate war, and yet men still die on battlefields because peace cannot be negotiated. All sane men agree that hungry children must be fed, but production lines often grow silent and children cry from hunger because negotiations between management and labor break down. All agree on the importance of good education, and yet many needed schools and recreational facilities go unbuilt because groups of people become deadlocked with inflexible differences of opinion. When the dispute becomes "a matter of principle or conscience," the difficulties are magnified immeasurably, as one often witnesses in another problematic area.

The Uncompromising Attitude of the Orthodox. The reluctant environment takes on new dimensions of resistance in the precincts of orthodoxy. But before one stands in critical judgment he must understand the logic of orthodoxy. "Orthodoxy" means "right opinion." The basic assumption of all orthodoxy is that truth and right are contained within its doctrine. When applied to life it establishes and preserves something that is uniquely precious. Hence, the changing scenes of nature and history must be made to conform to the eternal dogmas. The person who subscribes to the dogmas cannot compromise his "faith" without breaking his covenant with tradition, betraying his integrity, and perhaps even losing his identity.

There are obvious benefits and dangers in orthodoxy. The orthodox know who they are and what they believe. They can expend their entire efforts in achieving their goals rather than using their energies for periodic review of the relevance or reliability of their faith. Following the creed keeps one in the good graces of his fellow orthodox, and this gives both security and identity. On the other hand, orthodoxy necessarily presupposes and encourages protective isolation which robs one of the natural benefits of the continuously evolving processes of nature and history. The primary threat is stagnation, a serious weakness in times of creative advance. In the current revolutionary age the benefits and dangers of orthodoxy need careful review.

The Apathetic Attitude of the Uncommitted. Commitment presupposes conviction, and conviction presupposes that one alternative way of believing and behaving is better than all the others. In its doctrinal form this one alternative is characteristic of orthodoxy. But one clear consequence of the revolution of our times is the disintegration of the various types of orthodoxy. With the advances in communication and transportation, many people in different parts of the world are discovering that there are many different ways of thinking and acting. Careful examination and evaluation reveal that no one is clearly superior to all the others. Each has representatives that are both wise and sincere. The obvious result is that the informed citizen of the world must acknowledge that there are varieties of attitudes on every belief or action of man and that no one has been able to convince all his fellows that any one way is superior to all the others.

In the relativism that results, there are both advantages and hazards. On the one hand, and most evident, is the freedom of thought and action that is natural to relativism. This means that the individual or group is free to think through and experiment with any idea that seems to hold novel creative potential, and to do this without any fear of retaliation of any kind. In the midst of revolutionary change the significance of this opportunity can hardly be overemphasized. It is vital to novel, noble living. But, on the other hand, there is the hazard of apathy. If one is convinced that there are many different ways of believing and behaving, no one of which is clearly superior to all the others, what reason is there to embrace any one of them at any time? And yet the creative life demands direction and commitment, sometimes even to the point of sacrifice. Without it there is chaos. Hence, the apathetic attitude of the uncommitted, the extreme opposite of (and perhaps more dangerous than) the uncompromising attitude of the orthodox, is one of the obstacles to the secular christian mission.

The Tendency to Claim Personal Exemption. This obstacle may assume one of two basic forms. First, it may be an openly acknowledged conscientious objection. Just as there is a logic in both orthodoxy and relativism, so there is a logic here. The religious and political traditions of the Western world have honored the right of personal exemption on the basis of conscience and denounced any system of government which did not permit this form of behavior. Even in more severe cases where exacting consequences must be arranged by the appropriate authorities, there is still an assumed respect for any position that is taken on the basis of conscience. The dignity of the individual seems to demand this right. And yet there are obvious hazards in this. If honoring the conscientious objection jeopardizes the health or security of the entire community, the prerogatives of the community must prevail. This is serious and problematic.

A second form of the tendency to claim personal exemption is the sneaky dishonesty that goes contrary to the avowed obligations to the community or the state. There seems to be a natural temptation to cheat to one's advantage in an impersonal situation where there is no universal moral principle that is acknowledged by one and all as binding on one and all. Many citizens can rationalize dishonesty on income taxes with the spurious arguments that "everyone is doing it" and "no one is personally harmed by it." Who is the man who is not tempted to exempt himself from the statistics when they refer to the horrible consequences of one of his most precious habits? Or if the church is considered in error on the issues of birth control or censorship, is one not justified in a little selective cheating in bed or in the library? The fact is that every claim to personal exemption, whether honorably acknowledged or dishonestly concealed, is an obstacle to achieving some community-oriented goal and must be given appropriate careful thought.

The Curse of Structure Over Function. Closely related to the dangers of orthodoxy is the more general obstacle, the curse of structure over function. Throughout this study we have noted the interrelations of structure and function. If priority must be given, we have argued for the subordination of structure to function. The curse of the opposite approach can be illustrated in a number of ways. For example, the function of medicine, in both research and practice, is the elimination and prevention of disease. In our complex society, effective health programs often need some form of government sponsorship, but at that point national medical organizations label the efforts "socialized medicine" and lobbies effectively delay or prevent the programs while numbers of citizens have inadequate care. The same is often true in business. There is clear evidence that smoking is instrumental in a number of diseases, and yet the misleading advertising continues. Our factories, automobiles, and nuclear weapons continue to pollute the earth and its atmosphere while comparatively little is done about it. And when we die, we usually rob nature of the precious chemicals in our bodies by embalming them and sealing them in a vault. Our foolish burial customs subordinate the human function of the funeral to the barbaric commercial structure of the business of the funeral director. The legitimate and necessary functions of government today are too often lost in the elaboration of structure at the local, national, and international levels. The hands of the United Nations are too often tied with the twine of technicality. Some structure is essential, obviously, but that structure should depend upon a function in its relation to a felt need.

The Tendency to Despair. When one contemplates the many obstacles that can obstruct the secular christian mission, only a few of which are listed here, one cannot but ponder whether or not they are surmountable. One has to face the possibility that in combined form they may spell the ruin of man. Respected scientists, statesmen, and historians warn us of the real danger of the annihilation of life on the planet. The very fact that thousands of people can be casual about this threat in so brief a period of time may indicate another dimension of the danger. In the face of this, when hopes suffer prolonged frustration and common sense seems of no avail, there is a natural tendency to despair. And alas, despair is both a negative and a contagious attitude. It severs the nerve of endeavor, something that is vital to any mission, especially when the odds are unfavorable; and the contagious aspect only increases the odds against success. If this attitude is made to appear fashionable or sophisticated, the anxiety may disappear but the cause will be lost. Some other alternative must be forged, an alternative that is rooted in acknowledging the obstacles *as obstacles* and dealing with them accordingly.

3. The Challenge and the Response

The evolutionary processes in human behavior have brought the civilizations of earth to a crossroad. If the argument of the first chapter is sound, contemporary mankind is involved in a revolution that touches every part of human life. Never before in history have the alternatives of human destiny been so dreadful or so promising. On the one hand, man can continue to pollute the earth and render it uninhabitable; on the other hand, he can increase his disciplined research in the sciences and social sciences and the arts to build for himself a veritable paradise. To ponder the incredible advances in the various sciences—the transplantation of human organs, the creation of an artificial gene, the fantastic breakthrough in the use of computers and teaching machines, the amazing discoveries in the chemistry of learning, and many others—is to realize that we stand on the threshold of a new era. Whether the new era will be one of increasing cooperative fulfillment along international lines or one of total destruction on a planet scale remains to be seen. Obviously, the alternative of annihilation is preposterous beyond serious consideration. The other alternative is our only hope, and the one to explore.

The Challenge in the Challenge. Although the word "challenge" can be used in a variety of ways, in the present context it refers to a lure to accept a charge, a call to acknowledge a threat, a temptation to recognize and overcome an obstacle as an obstacle. In terms of the secular christian mission, the current challenge facing man is rooted in the double awareness of the urgency of the need for the mission on the one hand and the formidability of the obstacles on the other. Man has never faced a greater challenge.

Every genuine challenge holds both peril and promise. There is an element of danger and risk in man's attempt to deal with the threat; it arises out of the possibility of defeat. But it also provides man with the opportunity of instrumental good, namely, his pitting himself against the threat on the chances for success. In the realm of sports, each of the competing teams is willing to run the risk of defeat for the benefits of the game. The thrill of success is related directly to the measure of the challenge, without which there would be neither interest nor exertion. (It goes without saying that the rules of the game are such that each competing team finds the best practice to be the playing of the game, and the philosophy of bruising or destroying the opposing team is more appropriate to the battlefield than the gymnasium. Would that the contests of the former would be resolved in the latter with rules that are appropriate!)

Thus understood, every challenge is an invitation to enthusiastic and creative response. The adventuresome spirit of man has led to heroic responses in the past. Perhaps it will happen again.

The Creative Response. If our interpretation of challenge is reliable, the notion of a response is built in, so to speak. We have used such terms as "lure," "call," and "temptation." Basic to the meaning of each of these is the notion of some reaction. A lure entices; a call anticipates an answer; a temptation demands either yielding or resisting. Thus it can be said that every challenge has a built-in invitation to response.

A creative response is one that deals imaginatively and successfully with a challenge, transforming a problematic situation into an environment that is conducive to the greatest possible enrichment.[48] In general, a creative response to the challenges of our times must be guided by several pervading themes already identified in this study. First, that the basic clue to understanding the behavior of man is his quest for fulfillment. Man is guided and motivated by a "will to meaning" and one should not assume automatically, in cases of disagreement or conflict, that the contender is either ignorant or malevolent. Second, man is a multifaceted creature whose notion of the good life requires that the various basic needs be met. For this reason, he has designed societies with different institutions to meet the respective needs. Third, we need to cooperate with each other in order to save each other. We cannot remove the speck from our own eyes. And fourth, we need to bear in mind that the best preparation for any future good is the best good here and now. Both nature and history, as we have defined them, bear this out.

More specifically, the primary purpose of a creative response to the challenges of our times is the overcoming of the specific obstacles that stand in the way of the secular christian mission. Although we cannot expect all sincere and wise men to agree on either the goals or the means to the goals, we can and should expect all sincere and wise men to honor the established authority or the majority opinion and move on with dedication and enthusiasm. While we do not expect the orthodox to abandon their convictions forthwith, we do expect them to acknowledge that those who do not share their point of view may be equally wise and committed. By the same token, the committed have both the opportunity and the responsibility of attending the apathetic attitude of the uncommitted. The one who claims personal exemption, whether through publicly acknowledged conscientious objection or through secretive personal deviation, must be prepared to defend himself and/or take the consequences prescribed by law. And finally, each of us should examine anew the extent to which our personal and social conduct contributes to the curse of structure over function. While this does not exhaust the list of specific obstacles facing contemporary man, a widespread imaginative reaction to these areas of our common life would transform our current culture.

The key to the understanding of this study of salvation could well be focused upon the moment of creative response to the sequence of challenges. It is the focal point of purposive change. Indeed, all reform in the final analysis rests on that creative moment. When the challenge is great, so also is both the opportunity for reward and the danger of failure. The essential difference roots in the moment of response. If in the moment of need there is no christian response, there will be frustration instead of fulfillment, the deciding difference between good and evil, heaven and hell. In other words, in the final analysis it is the creative response that forever fashions the historic salvation event.

4. The Mission Accomplished

Since every mission is goal-oriented, the degree of success or failure is measured entirely in terms of the extent to which the goal is achieved. Obviously, if the obstacles that arise along the way cannot be overcome and the larger environment appropriately oriented, the mission will fail. On the other hand, with careful anticipation and preparation and creative responses along the way, the mission may be accomplished. There are two significant phases in a successful mission, the intrinsic benefits and the instrumental aspects.

The Intrinsic Benefits. Every salvation experience is an end in itself. It need not make an appeal to anything else to justify itself or give it meaning. This is so clearly a part of the total experience that no defense is required. It is simply appreciated for what it is; hence, its benefit is called intrinsic.

An accomplished mission has definite long-lasting benefits. There is an awareness of a task completed or an obligation discharged. If the mission has been necessary and honorable, its successful completion elicits an awareness of fulfillment that abides forever in the memory, giving increased satisfaction not only to a personal event but to history as well. If the mission has been a lifetime in the making, then its accomplishment is the crowning glory of a lifetime of dedication, the realization of a long-time dream. Nothing can change that one inspiring fact. This is salvation achieved.

The Instrumental Aspects. The intrinsic benefits of the mission accomplished escape the limitations of the momentary by participating in the ongoing evolutionary processes of nature and history. This is not to minimize the significance of the original experience or event. If the orginal event had never occurred there could be no long-term influence. But it is to point out that the larger meaning of any experience or event is realized by its becoming a guiding or controlling aspect in the continuing evolution of value. Unless it is renewed in the memory or utilized anew in the creative response it may well cease to be an identifiable influence in the current shaping of nature or history. Hence, the significance of the original event is measured in large part by the extent to which it functions in the prevailing pattern of development. The final points, separated into a separate section for the purpose of emphasis, continue this same theme.

5. The Mission Eternal

It will come as no surprise that this study is concluded with the notion of the mission eternal. The reason is not hard to find. The discussion of every key theme has tried to replace the older static-substance orientation with a dynamic-function interpretation. Every aspect of the quest for secular salvation finds its abiding meaning in creative development, and the *mission* as it is here defined is clearly the *quest* in its broadest conception. Thus any appropriate concluding remarks that adequately characterize the mission will probably have to review some of the basic clues in the earlier description of the quest.

The Meaning of "Eternal." The word "eternal" has a double meaning. In common parlance it means "everlasting." When applied to time, it refers backward as well as forward, implying such infinite duration as having neither beginning nor end. Since space and time can no longer be studied reliably in separation from each other, the same can be said of expansion through space as has been said of duration through time. In identifying the secular christian mission as eternal we are emphasizing the notion of the everlasting expansion in nature and history. This is a continuation of the notion of the instrumental aspects of the mission as accomplished. The word "eternal" may also refer to ultimacy in inherent quality. In the former usage, eternity defies measurement in terms of space-time; in this usage the reference is to inherent quality which is so ultimate in significance that it, too, defies measurement. The reference to "eternal life" in the Gospel of John seems to intend to include both of these meanings. This emphasis is a continuation of the notion of the intrinsic benefits of the mission accomplished. If we combine the notions of everlastingness and ultimacy, we lay the basis for the missionary hope.

The Missionary Hope. The first reaction to the notion of the mission as eternal may be one of distress in that it may appear to be an endless struggle against the obstacles that forever arise. But that is not the whole story. The preceding section suggests that the instrumental aspects are borne from the intrinsic benefits of a mission accomplished. The christ event, though often rooted in the soil of frustration or defeat, rises to a point where it justifies itself beyond the effort. The life of the secular church, often necessarily therapeutic in orientation, usually achieves such a fulfillment in sacrament and scripture that there is no calculation of the cost. The institutions of men arise out of human need, but when the secular community is christian the citizens no longer measure the return on their investment. Men fashion a notion of God only at great risk; yet, after the moment of encounter in the mode of "proper name," who would withhold the perilous commitment?

"Hope" refers to that state of being in which profound longing has a basis for satisfaction. It involves keen expectation with some assurance of attainment. There are occasions in life when it vies for the first place in the great trilogy—faith, hope, and love. In terms of the earlier discussion it is *hope* that makes the essential difference between heaven and hell, not that faith and love are irrelevant.

Man is a creature of hope, a species with a dream, a "will to meaning." To understand him aright is to acknowledge this. The dream may find fulfillment in any number of ways, and in as many ways it can be denied. To resist the creative process is to rob man of his future, while to commit oneself to it at every level and on every occasion of life is to come into a keen appreciation of christ, church, community, nature, history, and God. It is to enter the kingdom of heaven through the realization of the secular christian mission in the contemporary world.

Notes

1. Thomas J. J. Altizer, *The Gospel of Christian Atheism* (The Westminster Press, 1966), p. 26.

2. Harvey Cox, *The Secular City* (The Macmillan Company, 1965), p. 107.

3. John A. T. Robinson, *Honest to God* (The Westminster Press, 1963), Ch. 1; *The New Reformation?* (The Westminster Press, 1965), p. 10.

4. See Van A. Harvey, *A Handbook of Theological Terms* (The Macmillan Company, 1964), p. 239.

5. Thomas J. J. Altizer, "Creative Negation in Theology," *The Christian Century*, Vol. LXXXII (July 7, 1965), p. 866.

6. Thomas J. J. Altizer and William Hamilton, *Radical Theology and the Death of God* (The Bobbs-Merrill Company, Inc., 1966), p. 28.

7. *Ibid.*, p. ix.

8. Robinson, *The New Reformation?*, Ch. 3.

9. Gibson Winter, *The New Creation as Metropolis* (The Macmillan Company, 1963), p. 7.

10. *Ibid.*, pp. 58-59.

11. See Joseph Fletcher, *Situation Ethics: The New Morality* (The Westminster Press, 1966) and *Moral Responsibility: Situation Ethics at Work* (The Westminster Press, 1967).

12. Robinson, *The New Reformation?*, p. 21.

13. See J. S. Bezzant's chapter, "Intellectual Objections," in D. M. MacKinnon, *et al.*, *Objections to Christian Belief* (J. B. Lippincott Company, 1964), pp. 79–111.

14. *Ibid.*, pp. 15, 23, 50 ff., 66, and 105 respectively.

15. Stephen C. Pepper, *World Hypotheses: A Study in Evidence* (University of California Press, 1942).

16. See Mircea Eliade, *The Sacred and the Profane: The Nature of Religion* (Harper Torchbook, The Cloister Library, Harper & Row, Publishers, Inc., 1961), Chs. I and II.

17. Viktor E. Frankl, *Man's Search for Meaning* (Beacon Press, Inc., 1962), p. 99.

18. *Ibid.*, p. 103.

19. See Henry Nelson Wieman, *The Source of Human Good* (The University of Chicago Press, 1946) and *Man's Ultimate Commitment* (Southern Illinois University Press, 1958).

20. Vincent Taylor, *The Names of Jesus* (The Macmillan Company, 1962), p. 5.

21. See Joseph Klausner, *The Messianic Idea in Israel* (The Macmillan Company, 1955); Sigmund Mowinckel, *He That Cometh*, tr. by G. W. Anderson (Abingdon Press, 1956); and Helmer Ringgren, *The Messiah in the Old Testament* (London: SCM Press, Ltd., 1956).

22. See Reginald H. Fuller, *The Foundations of New Testament Christology* (Charles Scribner's Sons, 1965), Chs. II, III, and IV.

23. The literature on "the messianic consciousness of Jesus" is both too technical and too detailed for discussion here. Suffice it to say that Rudolf Bultmann and others are suspicious of messianic claims while T. W. Manson and others are not. See Bultmann's *Theology of the New Testament* (Charles Scribner's Sons, 1951), pp. 26–36, and Manson's *The Beginning of the Gospel* (London: Oxford University Press, 1950). Hugh Schonfield maintains not only that Jesus thought he was the messiah but that he staged the entire passion to prove it. See his *The Passover Plot* (Bernard Geis Associates, 1966). For a Jewish view which disagrees with this, see Samuel Sandmel, *We Jews and Jesus* (London: Oxford University Press, 1965). Vincent Taylor suggests that Jesus had little esteem for "current Messianic ideas and was never happy with the name 'Christ,'" and hence Professor Taylor feels that it is necessary to speak of "the Divine Consciousness of Jesus" rather than "the Messianic Consciousness of Jesus." See his *The Person of Christ in New Testament Teaching* (The Macmillan Company,

1959), pp. 156 ff. John Knox questions the relevance of the self-consciousness of Jesus in relation to the meaning of "Christ." See his *Criticism and Faith* (Abingdon-Cokesbury Press, 1952), p. 52.

24. Contrast Matt. 1:1–17 with Luke 3:23–38; Matt. 2:13–15 with Luke 2:21–23; Matt. 3:17 with Mark 1:11 and Luke 3:22; Matt. 4:1–11 with Luke 4:1–10; Matt. 6:9–13 with Luke 6:12–16 and Acts 1:13–14.

25. Oscar Cullmann, *The Christology of the New Testament*, Revised Edition, tr. by Shirley C. Guthrie and Charles A. M. Hall (The New Testament Library, The Westminster Press, 1964), pp. 199–203.

26. See Charles S. Braden, *Jesus Compared* (Prentice-Hall, Inc., 1957).

27. See Henry J. Cadbury, *The Peril of Modernizing Jesus* (Alec R. Allenson, Inc., 1962).

28. See Alfred North Whitehead, *Science and the Modern World* (The Macmillan Company, 1944) and *Religion in the Making* (The Macmillan Company, 1926).

29. *Oxford Universal Dictionary* (Oxford University Press, 1955).

30. Eliade, *The Sacred and the Profane*, p. 11.

31. Paul Tillich, *The Dynamics of Faith* (Harper Torchbook, The Cloister Library, Harper & Row, Publishers, Inc., 1957), pp. 41–54.

32. *Ibid.*, pp. 41–43.

33. Bultmann's meaning is not entirely clear and his proposal has led to an extensive debate. See Hans Werner Bartsch (ed.), *Kerygma and Myth: A Theological Debate* (Harper Torchbook, The Cloister Library, Harper & Brothers, 1961).

34. The same tendencies are found in the scriptures of other world religions. See, for example, Harry M. Buck, "From History to Myth: A Comparative Study," *The Journal of Bible and Religion*, Vol. XXIX (July, 1961), pp. 219–226.

35. Cox, *The Secular City*, pp. 182–183.

36. Robert Lee, *Religion and Leisure in America* (Abingdon Press, 1964), pp. 24–25.

37. Wieman, *Man's Ultimate Commitment*, p. 229.

38. Edgar S. Brightman, *A Philosophy of Religion* (Prentice-Hall, Inc., 1940), p. 134. Brightman's fifth chapter has been used here as a guide and all quotes in this section come from that chapter.

39. *Ibid.*, p. 140.

40. *Radical Theology and the Death of God*, pp. x–xi.

41. See Robert McAfee Brown, "What Does the Slogan Mean?" in Bernard Murchland (ed.), *The Meaning of the Death of God* (Vintage Books, Inc., 1967), pp. 170–184.

42. Harvey, *A Handbook of Theological Terms*, p. 108.

43. *Ibid.*, pp. 105–108.

44. See Alfred North Whitehead, *Process and Reality* (The Macmillan Company, 1929), p. 525.

45. See R. G. Collingwood, *The Idea of Nature* (Oxford University Press, 1945), especially Part III.

46. See Wieman, *Man's Ultimate Commitment*, p. 267.

47. For pro and con, see Harvey Cox, *The Secular City;* E. L. Mascall, *The Secularization of Christianity* (Holt, Rinehart and Winston, Inc., 1965); Ronald G. Smith, *Secular Christianity* (Harper & Row, Publishers, Inc., 1966); Paul M. van Buren, *The Secular Meaning of the Gospel* (The Macmillan Company, 1963); John J. Vincent, *Secular Christ* (Abingdon Press, 1968); and Colin Williams, *Faith in a Secular Age* (Harper & Row, Publishers, Inc., 1966).

48. See Wieman, *Man's Ultimate Commitment*, p. 4.